RAND NATIONAL DEFENSE RESEARCH INSTITUTE

The RAND Online Measure Repository for Evaluating Psychological Health and Traumatic Brain Injury Programs

The RAND Toolkit, Volume 2

Joie D. Acosta, Kerry A. Reynolds, Emily M. Gillen, Kevin Carter Feeney, Carrie M. Farmer, Robin M. Weinick

Prepared for the Office of the Secretary of Defense and the Defense Centers of Excellence for Psychological Health and Traumatic Brain Injury

This research was sponsored by the the Office of the Secretary of Defense (OSD) and the Defense Centers of Excellence for Psychological Health and Traumatic Brain Injury. It was conducted in the Forces and Resources Policy Center, a RAND National Defense Research Institute (NDRI) program. NDRI is a federally funded research and development center sponsored by the OSD, the Joint Staff, the Unified Combatant Commands, the Navy, the Marine Corps, the defense agencies, and the defense Intelligence Community under Contract W74V8H-06-C-0002.

Library of Congress Cataloging-in-Publication Data is available for this publication.

ISBN: 978-0-8330-5938-3

The RAND Corporation is a nonprofit institution that helps improve policy and decisionmaking through research and analysis. RAND's publications do not necessarily reflect the opinions of its research clients and sponsors.

Support RAND—make a tax-deductible charitable contribution at www.rand.org/giving/contribute.html

RAND® is a registered trademark.

RAND OFFICES
SANTA MONICA, CA • WASHINGTON, DC
PITTSBURGH, PA • NEW ORLEANS, LA • JACKSON, MS • BOSTON, MA
CAMBRIDGE, UK • BRUSSELS, BE
www.rand.org

Preface

Throughout the past decade, U.S. military forces have been engaged in extended conflicts in Iraq and Afghanistan. While most military personnel cope well across the deployment cycle, increases in stress associated with rapid operational tempo may raise the risk for mental health challenges. During this time, the U.S. Department of Defense (DoD) has implemented numerous programs to support service members and their families as they cope with these challenges. These programs address various components of biological, psychological, social, spiritual, and holistic influences on psychological health along the resilience, prevention, and treatment continuum and focus on a variety of clinical and nonclinical concerns. In response to this proliferation of programs, the Assistant Secretary of Defense for Health Affairs asked the RAND National Defense Research Institute (NDRI) to develop a set of tools to support ongoing assessment and evaluation of the DoD portfolio of programs that address psychological health and traumatic brain injury (TBI).

This report describes the development and uses of one of these tools, the RAND Online Measure Repository (ROMR). The ROMR is an online searchable database containing measures related to psychological health and TBI that was created to support monitoring and evaluation of such programs. This report describes the rationale, purpose, and uses of the ROMR, as well as the content of the repository itself. This report will be of particular interest to DoD officials responsible for programs related to psychological health and TBI, and should also be helpful for health policy officials within the U.S. Department of Veterans Affairs (VA) as well as others responsible for evaluating similar programs in nondefense-related settings. The ROMR is the second part of a toolkit that RAND is developing to support the evaluation of this DoD portfolio of programs. A link to the ROMR is available at the "Innovative Practices for Psychological Health and Traumatic Brain Injury" web page;[1] other tools in this series will be made available at this site as they are prepared.

This research was sponsored by the Office of the Secretary of Defense and the Defense Centers of Excellence for Psychological Health and Traumatic Brain Injury and conducted within the Forces and Resources Policy Center of the RAND National Defense Research Institute, a federally funded research and development center sponsored by the Office of the Secretary of Defense, the Joint Staff, the Unified Combatant Commands, the Navy, the Marine Corps, the defense agencies, and the defense Intelligence Community.

For more information on the RAND Forces and Resources Policy Center, see http://www.rand.org/nsrd/ndri/centers/frp.html or contact the director (contact information is provided on the web page).

---

[1] http://www.rand.org/multi/military/innovative-practices.html

Contents

Figure and Tables

Figure

Tables

Summary

More than 2.2 million service members have deployed to support military operations in Iraq and Afghanistan during the past decade (Levin, 2011). Among service members who had been deployed to Iraq and Afghanistan as of October 2007, approximately one-fifth reported current symptoms consistent with posttraumatic stress disorder (PTSD) or major depression, and about the same number reported having experienced a probable traumatic brain injury (TBI) while deployed (Tanielian and Jaycox, 2008). DoD has implemented numerous programs, interventions, and policies to address the increased concerns about PTSD and TBI and their effects on service members and their families. These programs focus on reducing the incidence of mental health problems via efforts to improve readiness and resilience; providing information, connecting individuals to care, and encouraging help seeking; identifying individuals with mental health concerns or TBI; providing or improving clinical services, or offering mental health services in nontraditional locations to expand access to care; providing a wide range of training and educational activities; and supporting service members and their families during times of military transition (Weinick et al., 2011).

As these efforts have proliferated, it has become increasingly important to evaluate their effectiveness. To support the design and implementation of such program evaluations, we developed an online repository of measures (the RAND Online Measures Repository, or ROMR) that indexes and describes measures related to psychological health and TBI that have been used in both civilian and military populations. Specifically, we identified measures of primary importance to TBI including measures of cognition, executive functioning, and memory. We have also identified measures of primary importance to psychological health in the following domains: PTSD, depression, anxiety, suicidal ideation, and resiliency. We also identified measures relevant to military units such as unit cohesion and force readiness and preservation.

The ROMR is the second part of a toolkit that RAND is developing to support the assessment and evaluation of the DoD portfolio of programs. A link to the ROMR is available at the "Innovative Practices for Psychological Health and Traumatic Brain Injury" web page;[1] other tools in this series will be made available at this site as they are prepared.

Focus of This Report

This report describes the ROMR, and explains how it was developed and how it can be used. Chapter One introduces the report by describing the need for an online searchable database

---

[1] http://www.rand.org/multi/military/innovative-practices.html

of measures to support monitoring and evaluation of psychological health and TBI programs. Chapter Two describes the development of the ROMR, including the rationale for its creation and the method used to identify measures and extract relevant information. Chapter Three provides a description of the measures included in the ROMR. Chapter Four describes the potential benefits of the ROMR to agency officials, program managers, mental health professionals, and those interested in program evaluation.

How the RAND Online Measure Repository Was Developed

The ROMR was developed using a series of literature searches, journal reviews, and expert recommendations to identify measures of anxiety, depression, PTSD, resiliency, suicidal thoughts, unit cohesion, force readiness and preservation, and measures related to TBI. Relevant articles were coded using a standardized abstraction procedure guided by supporting documents (e.g., glossary of terms) and procedures (weekly discussion of coding issues). We focused on sources that described the development, validation, and/or psychometric properties of one or more measures. From each source, we abstracted information about the measure's domains, administration, scoring, length, acquisition, and psychometric properties, as well as identified the populations to which the measure had been applied. Once information on measures was abstracted and reviewed, the database used for coding was converted into a searchable online tool.

Measures Included in the RAND Online Measure Repository

We identified 174 measures including a wide array of measures of depression (71), PTSD (49), and anxiety (41). Several measures related to exposure to traumatic events (21), stress and coping (16), resiliency (15), suicidal thoughts (16), and TBI (e.g., cognition functioning and speech) (20) were also identified. Fewer measures of force readiness (4) and unit cohesion (10) were identified, suggesting that this may be a less developed field of measurement. Eighty-four percent of the measures identified had been used with adults, and 23 percent had been used with children. The majority of measures were self-administered questionnaires. It is important to note that the purpose of the ROMR is to support program evaluation, rather than clinical care, so we have not included measures related to diagnosis of mental health disorders or TBI.

The measures most commonly used with military populations were those related to depression and PTSD. However, only about half of the total measures identified had ever been used with a military population. Additional work is needed to validate many of these measures in military populations, especially measures with clinical significance, no-cost measures of anxiety, and measures for evaluation of programs related to TBI. As updates are made to the ROMR, additions may also be considered to continue building areas of the ROMR where fewer measures were identified. These areas include measures of leadership, force readiness, unit cohesion, and family support.

Potential Uses of the RAND Online Measure Repository

The ROMR has a number of potential uses across a wide variety of programs and professionals.

Select Measures for Program Evaluation or Research Related to Psychological Health and Traumatic Brain Injury

The primary purpose of the ROMR is to help program evaluators select appropriate measures for use. Program evaluators, researchers, and those responsible for program implementation can use the repository to identify specific measures across a wide variety of domains related to TBI including cognition, executive functioning, and memory, and psychological health including depression, anxiety, PTSD, stress and coping, and resiliency, among others.

Select Measures for Dual Use by Both Clinicians and Program Evaluators or Researchers

The ROMR includes information on available clinical cutoff scores used to determine when individuals require clinical services, to inform clinical case planning, or to screen individuals who may be at risk for developing a psychological disorder. Measures with clinical meaning may be useful to both clinicians providing novel interventions or other services specifically targeting clinical outcomes and to the evaluators or researchers working with these clinicians to determine the effectiveness of their services.

Identify Core Outcome Measures for Evaluating Similar Programs

Organizations or individuals responsible for a group of programs could consider using the ROMR to identify and endorse a specific set of outcome measures that are both reliable and valid for the populations served across a variety of domains. Endorsing a specific set of outcome measures could allow for consistency in tracking core outcomes or indicators of effectiveness across an array of programs.

Determine Need for Additional Reliability and Validity Testing of Measures with Military Populations

The ROMR's assessment of measures currently used by program evaluators and researchers can be helpful in determining where more work needs to be done to establish reliability and validity of measures with military populations. Additional psychometric development is particularly important for domains such as force readiness, where only a few measures exist, and domains such as anxiety, where there has been little testing with military populations.

Conclusion

Valid and reliable measures of psychological health and TBI-related constructs are needed to be able to monitor and evaluate programs that address these issues. The ROMR is a valuable tool that responds to this need by providing an online and searchable database of measures related to psychological health and TBI.

Acknowledgments

We gratefully acknowledge the assistance of the researchers on the RAND Innovative Practices in Psychological Health team who contributed to the identification and selection of domains for the RAND Online Measure Repository: Ellen Beckjord, Michael Fisher, Laurie Martin, Todd Helmus, Lisa Jaycox, and Deborah Scharf. We also thank those who provided administrative support, technical support, and other assistance in preparing both the online repository and technical report, including Michelle Horner, Kate Barker, Nick Salcedo, Monica Hertzman, Kiet Lieng, Lee Floyd, Christopher Fields, Reema Singh, Brian Stucky, and Cord Thomas. We are especially grateful to Brett Litz and Grant Marshall for reviewing earlier versions of this report. We also thank our current and past project monitors at the Defense Centers of Excellence for Psychological Health and Traumatic Brain Injury, Col Christopher Robinson and CAPT Edward Simmer, as well as Dr. Wendy Tenhula, for their support of our work.

Abbreviations

DCoE	Defense Centers of Excellence for Psychological Health and Traumatic Brain Injury
DoD	U.S. Department of Defense
GAO	U.S. Government Accountability Office
PTSD	posttraumatic stress disorder
ROMR	RAND Online Measure Repository
TBI	traumatic brain injury

CHAPTER ONE

Introduction

Our nation's all-volunteer military force continues to endure the longest era of conflict in its history. The past decade has been characterized by frequent deployments and exposure to combat-related trauma, which have increased the risk of postdeployment psychological health problems among the more than 2.2 million troops that have deployed since 2001 (Levin, 2011). Concerns have been raised about the incidence of posttraumatic stress disorder (PTSD), major depression, traumatic brain injury (TBI), and suicide among returning service members. Research has shown that between 15 and 20 percent of returning service members reported symptoms consistent with current PTSD or major depression. Similarly, about 20 percent reported having experienced a probable TBI while deployed (Tanielian and Jaycox, 2008). These medical and psychological health issues affect both service members and their families (Tanielian and Jaycox, 2008; Chandra et al., 2010).

In response to growing concerns about the effects of deployment on service members, the Department of Defense (DoD) Task Force on Mental Health recommended that DoD implement an array of programs to address emerging psychological health issues (Department of Defense Task Force on Mental Health, 2007). In response to these recommendations, DoD has implemented programs, interventions, and policies to improve readiness and resilience, to improve awareness and understanding of psychological health issues and TBI, and to increase access to care and enhance existing services. Programs and interventions focus on:

- identifying individuals with psychological health issues or TBI
- encouraging help-seeking behavior
- providing support to service members during times of military transition
- providing or enhancing existing clinical services programs
- providing care in nontraditional locations
- providing training and education activities to improve the capacity of mental health providers. (Weinick et al., 2011)

To help DoD appropriately monitor the effectiveness of these programs, we developed the RAND Online Measure Repository (ROMR) to increase the information available on measures that can support program evaluation in these areas. The ROMR is the second part of a toolkit that RAND is developing to support the evaluation of the DoD portfolio of programs. A link to the ROMR is available at the "Innovative Practices for Psychological Health and Traumatic Brain Injury" web page;[1] other tools in this series will be made available at this site as they are prepared.

The Need for a Repository of Measures on Psychological Health and Traumatic Brain Injury to Evaluate Military Programs

The U.S. Government Accountability Office (GAO) defines program evaluation as individual systematic studies conducted periodically or on an ad hoc basis to "assess whether the program works . . . and identify adjustments that may improve its results" (GAO, 2005, p. 3). The purpose of program evaluation is to determine if a program is a worthwhile investment and is achieving its intended impact, and to provide accountability to program funders and the public. Ongoing evaluation can serve as an early warning system for program funders to identify adjustments to program approaches that may improve their results.

Although program evaluations may take many forms, a key piece of any evaluation design is the careful selection of measures that are appropriate for the population served by the program (e.g., service members and spouses or children of service members) and for the outcomes being targeted for improvement (e.g., reducing depression, building resiliency). Measures assess "the type or level of program activities conducted (process), the direct products and services delivered by a program (outputs), and/or the results of those products and services (outcomes)" and can be in the format of a questionnaire or inventory, structured or unstructured interview, or observation rating tool (GAO, 2005, p. 4).

One key challenge in conducting rigorous evaluations is identifying and selecting appropriate evaluation measures. The creation of a single database of potential measures with information about their use can support program evaluation activities by reducing the burden on program staff to identify and select appropriate measures.

Existing measure repositories are limited because they lack information on whether measures have been used with a military population, do not include measures related to TBI, or require a fee for usage (Chapter Two contains a review of existing repositories). To address these issues and support the design and implementation of evaluations of psychological health and TBI programs, we developed the ROMR. This publicly available online repository indexes and describes measures related to psychological health and TBI that have been used in both civilian and military populations, as well as measures that are specifically relevant to military units (e.g., unit cohesion, force readiness and preservation). We identified measures of primary importance to TBI including measures of cognition, executive functioning, and memory. We have also included measures of primary importance to psychological health in the domains of PTSD, depression, anxiety, military unit measures, suicidal ideation, and resiliency. It is important to note that the purpose of the ROMR is to support program evaluation, rather than clinical care, so we have not included measures related to diagnosis of TBI.

The ROMR contains 174 measures related to psychological health and TBI, including descriptions of each measure, information about their development and uses (e.g., whether they have been used with a military population), as well as documentation on their reliability and validity and other characteristics (e.g., length of measure, cost). Measure descriptions are indexed using an online interface (accessible at the "Innovative Practices" web page) that allows

---

[1] http://www.rand.org/multi/military/innovative-practices.html

repository users to search for specific measures based on content-relevant keywords or other characteristics of each measure (e.g., whether the measure has published psychometrics) and to compare measures side by side. Users can search by keyword or other features and can conduct side-by-side comparisons of measures to identify the best options for use in program evaluation. The ROMR provides a targeted, user-friendly tool to support the design and implementation of evaluations of new or existing programs related to psychological health and TBI. The online interface is intended as the most useful way to access the cataloged information about each measure.

This report provides documentation on the ROMR to help potential users understand its creation and to explain how it can be used. Chapter 2 describes the development of the ROMR, including the method we followed in identifying measures and extracting relevant information. Chapter 3 provides a description of the measures included in the ROMR. Chapter 4 describes the potential benefits of the ROMR to agency officials, program managers, mental health professionals, and those interested in program evaluation.

A series of appendixes specifies the contents of the ROMR, provides additional detail on the development of ROMR, and includes supporting materials to aid potential users. Appendix A contains a brief description of existing measure repositories that were reviewed to inform the development of the ROMR. Appendix B describes the detailed literature search strategies used to identify relevant measures. Appendix C displays a comprehensive list of the references consulted in developing the ROMR, and Appendix D lists the measures included in the ROMR. Appendix E describes in detail how information on each measure was abstracted by RAND staff, and Appendix F contains a glossary of relevant terms. Appendix G provides information to help users interpret reliability and validity information contained in the ROMR. Finally, a brief guide for how to access and search the ROMR comprises Appendix H. Complete information on each measure included in the ROMR is available at the "Innovative Practices" web page.

CHAPTER TWO

Development of the RAND Online Measure Repository

The first step in developing the ROMR was to conduct a search of existing measure repositories, which were identified through a web-based search as well as personal communication with experts in the fields of psychological measurement and military mental health. This process identified eight repositories that contained measures related to TBI, psychological health at the individual or unit level, or resiliency: the ADAI Substance Use Assessment Instrument Library; the Buros Institute of Mental Measurements; the Center for Outcome Measurement in Brain Injury; the Compendium of Assessment and Research Tools; the ETS Test Collection/Carl C. Brigham Library; Measuring Violence-Related Attitudes, Behaviors, and Influences Among Youths: A Compendium of Assessment Tools, 2nd ed.; the National Center for the Study of PTSD; and the Patient Reported Outcome and Quality of Life Instruments Database.

We reviewed the eight existing repositories to determine the type of measures they included and examined several features, including access fees, inclusion of measures used with military populations, information about obtaining measures, and psychometric properties described by the repositories. We found that each had a number of challenges that would limit its potential direct use for evaluating military programs. For example, some repositories included information on how to obtain the measure or the psychometric qualities of the measure, but did not contain information on whether the measure had been used with a military population. We could not locate a repository that included a combination of measures related to TBI, psychological health at both the individual and unit levels, and resiliency, and we found only one repository that contained information about whether the measures had been used with a military population. Furthermore, many military programs focus on improving the psychological health of military family members, but it was difficult to find measures for both adults and children within many of the existing repositories. Appendix A describes the existing measure repositories in greater detail.

Developed to address the limitations of existing repositories, the ROMR differs from other available databases in the content area covered, populations targeted, and the audience for which it was designed. The ROMR focuses on measures related to TBI for adults and measures related to psychological health for adults, adolescents, and children in both civilian and military populations. In addition, while existing databases may provide some content free of charge, the entire content of the ROMR is publicly available at no cost. Finally, the ROMR is designed for the purpose of program evaluation, with measures focused on outcomes relevant to TBI including cognition, executive functioning, and memory, and measures focused on mental health, including depression, PTSD, and resiliency. These features are designed to improve user-friendliness and efficiency by reducing the examination of less relevant materials and increasing quick identification of the most relevant measures. Table 2.1 compares ROMR features to other existing measure repositories.

Once we determined the required features of the ROMR, we began a systematic process to identify measures related to TBI, psychological health, unit cohesion, and resiliency needed to populate the repository.

Identifying Potential Measures

We searched the peer-reviewed literature to identify measures of anxiety, depression, PTSD, TBI (e.g., cognition, executive functioning, memory), resiliency, suicidal thoughts, unit

Table 2.1
Key Features of ROMR Compared to Other Repositories

Key Features	Allows search for measures used with military populations	Free	Includes information on how to obtain the measure	Includes psychometric qualities of measure	Includes multiple measures of psychological health (individual level)	Includes measures of psychological health (unit level)	Includes measures related to TBI	Includes measures of resiliency
RAND Online Measure Repository	✓	✓	✓	✓	✓	✓	✓	✓
ADAI Substance Use Assessment Instrument Library		✓	✓	✓				
Buros Institute of Mental Measurements			✓	✓	✓			
Center for Outcome Measurement in Brain Injury		✓	✓				✓	
Compendium of Assessment and Research Tools (CART)		✓	✓		✓			
ETS Test Collection/ Carl C. Brigham Library			✓	✓	✓		✓	
Measuring Violence-Related Attitudes, Behaviors, and Influences Among Youths: A Compendium of Assessment Tools, 2nd ed.		✓	✓	✓	✓			
National Center for the Study of PTSD	✓	✓	✓		✓			
Patient Reported Outcome and Quality of Life Instruments Database (ProQolid)		Free for basic/ Fee for advanced		Advanced version only	✓			✓

cohesion,[1] and force health readiness.[2] To identify relevant articles, we began with keyword searches of content-relevant databases, followed by title and abstract review. Additional measures were identified during article abstraction and by content-area experts. We focused on sources that described the development, validation, and/or psychometric properties of one or more measures.

Literature Search

We conducted keyword searches in three databases that focus on substantive areas pertaining to mental health and psychology, medicine, and traumatic stress: PsychINFO (psychology), PubMed (medicine), and the Published International Literature on Traumatic Stress database (PILOTS, traumatic stress). We also searched for articles published in the last two years in the journal *Military Psychology*.

Multiple searches were conducted in each database to ensure that references from all relevant substantive domains were included. We restricted our search to articles published in English during or after 2000, and excluded editorials, letters, and commentaries. Search strategies varied for each substantive domain and were based on the constraints of each electronic database. However, most searches were variations on a basic three-category format: The first category focused on keywords related to the substantive domain, the second category focused on keywords relevant for establishing psychometric properties, and the third category focused on keywords related to the measurement techniques relevant to that domain. Details of the search strategies can be viewed in Appendix B, and an example follows in Table 2.2.

Expert Consultation

The content area for some of the measures included in the repository represent emerging areas of research—specifically, unit cohesion and force health readiness. For these areas, content area experts were asked to identify additional relevant articles or measures that may not have been identified in initial literature searches.

Review of References

Additional articles and measures were identified by reviewing the references in articles identified for inclusion in the repository.

Selecting Measures from the Literature Search to Include in the Repository

Title and Abstract Review

From the list of articles identified during our literature search, we reviewed titles to remove those that were clearly irrelevant to the current project. For the remaining articles, we reviewed

---

[1] Unit cohesion is defined as the bonding together of members of an organization in such a way as "to sustain their will and commitment to each other, their unit and the mission" (Powell et al., 2006).

[2] Force health readiness is defined as the ability of U.S. military forces to "optimize and protect the psychological and physical health of service members and their families through policies and programs across all phases of deployment." Force health protection and readiness is also referred to as force protection, force preservation, or force preservation and readiness (Office of the Deputy Assistant Secretary of Defense, 2011).

Table 2.2
Keyword Categories: Example Search Strategy for TBI Articles in PubMed

Category 1: Substantive Domain	Category 2: Psychometric Properties	Category 3: Measurement Techniques	
• traumatic brain injury	• validation studies as topic [MeSH] • valid* • reliab*	• survey • surveys • instrument • instruments • questionnaire • questionnaires • psychiatric status rating scales • measure • measures	• psychometrics • aptitude tests • digit span • language tests • hearing tests • neuropsychological tests • retention [MeSH] • psychomotor performance • sociometric techniques

NOTE: The asterisk (*) denotes a wildcard search. MeSH is an abbreviation for medical subject heading.

abstracts and categorized articles into three groups: articles that were clearly irrelevant (e.g., addressed a topic area not covered in the ROMR), articles that should move forward to full-text review, and those that were questionable. Questionable articles were discussed among the team and a decision was made to include or exclude them. An electronic record of inclusion and exclusion criteria was updated as decisions were made.

Full-Text Review for Inclusion and Exclusion Criteria

Articles identified for full-text review were carefully examined for information relevant to inclusion and exclusion criteria. Articles that met inclusion criteria were then coded according to the process outlined in Table 2.3.

Articles Identified During the Literature Search

The database searches and review of *Military Psychology* yielded 2,083 unique sources. Title review excluded 1,350 articles. Of 733 articles that underwent abstract review, 471 were excluded. Another 80 articles were excluded during full-text review. The title and full-text reviews to determine inclusion/exclusion were conducted by a librarian, two research assistants, and two RAND researchers with expertise in psychology, economics, and health policy. The primary reason for exclusion during full-text review was that the article addressed a foreign population, which typically was not revealed in the title or abstract. All remaining articles (n = 290) were included in the review. A flowchart depicting the identification and exclusion of references is shown in Figure 2.1.

Although 290 articles were ultimately included, multiple articles often addressed the psychometric properties of a single measure. Furthermore, some articles contained information about multiple measures. The final ROMR contains 174 measures. Appendix C contains a list of the articles reviewed, and Appendix D contains a list of the unique measures included in the database.

Table 2.3
Inclusion and Exclusion Criteria

Inclusion Criteria

- Contained a reference to at least one of the following eight domains:
  1. Depression, including dysthymia, anhedonia, bipolar disorder, cyclothymia, and bereavement but excluding postpartum depression
  2. Anxiety, including general anxiety, social anxiety, obsessive compulsive disorder, panic disorder, phobias, and worry but excluding specific anxieties such as fear of pain, fear of death, fear of hospitalization, etc.
  3. PTSD, including measures of exposure to trauma, internalizing and externalizing behaviors associated with trauma, symptoms of PTSD, acute stress reaction, acute stress disorder, combat and operational stress reaction, reexperiencing traumatic events, avoidance of place/things reminiscent of trauma, emotional numbing, and increased arousal
  4. TBI, including diagnosis of insults, head injuries, head trauma, closed head wounds, concussions, and other acquired brain trauma, cognitive and motor abilities
  5. Suicidal thoughts, including ideations, intent, and fantasies
  6. Resiliency, including coping with stress and hardiness
  7. Force health readiness
  8. Unit cohesion, including unit support.

- Addressed some aspect of psychometric evaluation of the focus measure (e.g., calculation of scale reliability, test of validity)

- Focused on one or more of the following three subpopulations: (1) U.S. and limited international military populations; (2) major U.S. racial/ethnic groups (e.g., white, African American, Latino American, etc.); (3) general inpatient populations at hospitals, psychiatric hospitals and rehabilitation facilities. Search parameters were extended to include British, Canadian, Australian, and Israeli military populations because there was limited literature on U.S. military populations.

Exclusion Criteria

- Editorials, letters, and commentaries

- Published in a language other than English

- Focused solely on international populations with the exception of British, Canadian, Australian, and Israeli military populations

- Focused solely on individuals over age 50 or retirees, as well as studies where the sample population had a mean age of 50 or above. The majority of active duty service members are under 50, consequently measures created for use with individuals over 50 would not be applicable to the majority of active duty service members.

- Examined a specialized subpopulation (e.g., cancer patients with depression, patients with chronic pain, or specific inpatient populations)

- Addressed TBI solely in children under 18 because TBI is an injury primarily acquired by service members in theater, not their children.

Abstracting Consistent Information on Each Measure

Article Coding and Data Abstraction

The first two authors and two coders abstracted the information necessary for populating the ROMR from each included article. Each piece of abstracted information represents a characteristic or quality of the measure that potential users might find helpful during measure selection. Abstracted information included the following:

- **Substantive domains:** as many domains as were relevant to the measure; for example, a measure assessing symptoms of both anxiety and depression

Figure 2.1
Flow Chart for Literature Search

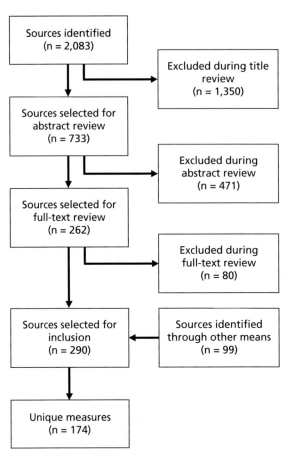

NOTE: More than one measure may be addressed in a single article, and more than one article may address a specific measure.
RAND *RR487z2-2.1*

- **Populations:** information about the age groups (adult or child) with which the measure has been used and whether or not the measure has been used with a military population
- **Measure administration:** including the method of administration (e.g., questionnaire, interview), the person who administers the measure (e.g., self, trained clinician), and the respondent (e.g., self, caregiver)
- **Scoring:** information about subscales, response options, and the presence or absence of a clinical cutoff score
- **Measure length:** number of items in the measure
- **Psychometric properties:** including reports of reliability and validity
- **Measure developer:** information about who developed the measure and the reference for the original publication of the measure if available

- **Measure acquisition:** how to obtain the measure and if there is a fee to obtain or use the measure.

Further detail on abstracted information is available in the data abstraction form in Appendix E.

Procedure for Coding Articles

Coders received initial instruction on the use of the data abstraction form and content to be included for each domain of interest, and then each coded five articles, which were reviewed by this report's first two authors. This process was repeated until the coders successfully coded articles independently and with a high degree of reliability among team members. The team regularly reviewed questions about coding; Appendix F is a glossary of terms developed by the team to support the coding effort. Once all articles were coded, the first two authors reviewed all measure descriptions for completeness of information and clarity.

During this review, we found that while the search strategy identified a wide range of measures currently in use, it failed to yield psychometric information for 55 of the measures and did not adequately distinguish whether each of these measures had ever been used by a military population for over half of the measures. To augment these two domains, authors engaged the existing team and a quantitative psychologist with expertise in psychometrics to conduct a second, more targeted search of the same databases used in the initial search strategy, relaxing the inclusion and exclusion criteria. To locate additional psychometric information on measures for which information was missing, a search was conducted using the name of the measure and the keywords *reliability, validity,* and *psychometrics.* To augment information on whether each measure had ever been used with a military population, the team conducted additional literature searches using keywords including the name of the measure and *Army, Navy, Marine Corps, Air Force, service member,* and *military.* This targeted search produced additional information that allowed us to determine, for all measures, whether they had ever been used with a military population. We collected additional information about use with a military population for 47 measures, and about psychometric evidence for an additional 43 measures. The final set of all entries can be viewed in the online ROMR, at the "Innovative Practices" web page.

CHAPTER THREE

Characteristics of Measures in the RAND Online Measure Repository

We identified 174 measures including a wide array of measures of depression (71), PTSD (49), and anxiety (41). Several measures related to exposure to traumatic events (21), stress and coping (16), resiliency (15), suicidal thoughts (16), and TBI (20) were also identified. Fewer measures of force readiness (4) and unit cohesion (10) were identified, suggesting that this may be a less developed field of measurement. Eighty-four percent of the measures identified had been used with adults, and 23 percent had been used with children.

In this chapter, we describe the characteristics of the measures included in the ROMR based on their use in military populations, availability (cost), breadth (covering a single domain or multiple) and length, mode of administration, clinical significance, and psychometrics. Appendix D contains a complete list of the measures included in the repository.

Use by Military Populations and Cost

Two features of the repository are particularly useful for evaluating programs for military populations. First, determining whether a measure has been used in military populations shows that it has been tested already as directly applicable to those populations. Second, understanding whether there is a cost associated with using a particular measure can help researchers and program evaluators plan for resources that may be needed to use the measure. Programs with more limited resources may wish to select measures that are available at no cost.

Table 3.1 summarizes the number of measures, by domain, that have been used with military populations, and the number available at no cost. As previously mentioned, measures of depression (54), PTSD (33), and anxiety (26) were among the most common measures identified and were frequently available at no cost. Similarly, measures of depression and PTSD were the most commonly used with military populations. Although only 10 measures of unit cohesion were identified, as expected, all had been used with military populations.

Breadth and Length

When selecting measures for program evaluation, program staff must often balance the length of time required or the space on a questionnaire needed to use a measurement instrument against the ability to capture multiple outcomes of interest. Some efficiencies may be gained by using a single measure that has subscales to specifically assess well-being in multiple domains.

Table 3.1
Measures Identified for Military Populations and Available at No Cost, by Domain

Domain	Number of Measures Identified	Number of Measures Used with Military Populations	Number of Measures Available at No Cost
PTSD	49	36	33
Depression	71	31	54
Anxiety	41	18	26
TBI	20	13	8
Suicidal thoughts	16	7	7
Resiliency	15	10	10
Stress and coping	16	10	10
Exposure to traumatic events	21	15	15
Force readiness	4	4	3
Unit cohesion	10	10	7

NOTE: Measures can cover more than one domain; therefore, numbers in this table do not represent unique measures and the table columns cannot be summed. Multiple versions of a single measure (e.g., a two-item version and a one-item version) were counted as unique measures.

Of the measures included in the ROMR, 30 percent address two or more domains (e.g., depression and anxiety), with the remainder of measures addressing a single domain (e.g., depression). Table 3.2 summarizes both the total number of measures covering one, two, three, or four or more domains, and the mean number of items for each type of measure. As expected, measures covering a single domain typically consisted of fewer items than measures covering two or more domains, although there was wide variability.

Table 3.2
Measures Covering Multiple Domains

Number of Domains Covered by Measure	Number of Measures Identified	Number of Items		
		Mean	Standard Deviation	Range
1	122	22.50	26.5	1–169
2	31	38.10	31.5	2–120
3	14	58.21	66.4	6–207
4+	7	220.70	223.2	5–567

Methods of Administration

Ensuring that programs have appropriate staff to administer measures is another key factor to consider when selecting evaluation measures. Some measures can only be administered through an interview or via observation by a clinician or trained professional. For that reason, many program evaluators select measures that are self-administered through pen-and-paper or online assessments. Table 3.3 summarizes both the measure administrator and the method of administration for the measures included in the ROMR. The majority of measures identified were self-administered questionnaires. Over half of these had been used with military populations.

Clinical Significance

Programs providing novel interventions or other services specifically targeting clinical outcomes may need measures that provide information useful for both program evaluation and clinical case planning or for screening of at-risk individuals. About one-fifth of the measures in the ROMR have clinical cutoff scores used to assign clinical meaning to an individual's responses. Table 3.4 summarizes the domains captured by measures in the ROMR with clini-

Table 3.3
Methods Used to Administer Measures

Administration of Measures	Number of Measures Identified	Number of Measures Used with Military Populations
Administrator		
Self-administered	127	75
Administered by clinician	25	13
Administered by trained professional or staff member	30	17
Other	12	6
Method		
Survey questionnaire (pen and paper)	125	76
Survey questionnaire (online)	14	8
Structured interview	16	6
Semi-structured interview	18	7
Other	22	13

NOTE: A single measure could be available in both pen-and-paper and online questionnaire formats; therefore, the numbers in this table do not represent unique measures. Multiple versions of a single measure (e.g., a two-item version and a one-item version) are counted as unique measures.

Table 3.4
Measures with Clinical Significance Scores, by Domain

Domain	Number of Measures with Clinical Cutoff Scores	Number of Measures with Clinical Cutoff Scores and Used with Military Populations
PTSD	24	17
Depression	12	5
Anxiety	10	5
TBI	4	4
Suicidal thoughts	5	4
Stress and coping	2	2
Exposure to traumatic events	3	3

NOTE: Measures can cover more than one domain; therefore, numbers in this table do not represent unique measures and the table columns cannot be summed. Multiple versions of a single measure (e.g., a two-item version and a one-item version) are counted as unique measures. Resiliency, force readiness, and unit cohesion are excluded from this table because they are not clinical measures.

cal cutoff scores, among which PTSD and depression are the most common. We were able to identify only a limited number of measures with clinical significance scores that had been used with military populations; however, 17 measures of PTSD have clinical cutoff scores and have been used with military populations.

Psychometrics

The presence of published psychometrics can be an important indicator of the extent to which the measure assesses the intended construct, and does so in a manner that can be repeated across multiple administrations or for different types of respondents. When searching the ROMR database for available measures, program evaluators may wish to consider only measures that have published psychometric information, as this could help narrow a search strategy to include only the most established measures. This is especially important if the evidence gathered during program evaluation efforts will be used to effect change within a program, making it essential that collected information accurately reflects the desired constructs. The ROMR includes specific information that describes the reliability and/or validity of each instrument described in published work, as well as a short primer to help users interpret this information (Appendix G). Table 3.5 provides a summary of measures for which information on *both* the reliability and validity of the measure was available in the identified literature. There are fewer measures with published psychometric information that have been validated with military populations, and even fewer that are available at no cost. Additional work is needed to validate many of these measures in military populations, especially no-cost measures of anxiety and measures related to TBI.

Table 3.5
Measures with Published Psychometrics, by Domain

Measures	Number of Measures Identified	Number of Measures Used with Military Populations	Number of Measures Used with Military Populations and Available at No Cost
PTSD	49	36	25
Depression	71	31	20
Anxiety	41	18	7
TBI	20	13	4
Suicidal thoughts	16	7	3
Resiliency	15	10	5
Stress and coping	16	10	5
Exposure to traumatic events	21	15	10
Force readiness	4	4	3
Unit cohesion	10	10	7

NOTE: Measures can cover more than one domain; therefore, numbers in this table do not represent unique measures and the table columns cannot be summed. Multiple versions of a single measure (e.g., a two-item version and a one-item version) are counted as unique measures. Published psychometrics includes data on both the reliability and validity of the measure.

CHAPTER FOUR

Potential Uses of the RAND Online Measure Repository

The ROMR has a number of potential uses across a wide variety of programs and by diverse groups of professionals. This chapter provides more detail on how the ROMR can be used by program evaluators, researchers, clinicians, and others interested in measuring psychological health and constructs related to TBI. Appendix H provides a more detailed user guide with specific instructions about how to access and search the ROMR.

Select Measures for Program Evaluation or Research Related to Psychological Health and Traumatic Brain Injury

The primary purpose of the ROMR is to help researchers and program evaluators select appropriate measures based on the needs of their program and the population it serves. Researchers, program evaluators, and others can use the repository to identify specific measures across a wide variety of domains related to psychological health, including depression, anxiety, PTSD, stress and coping, and resiliency. The ROMR also includes measures related to TBI. Besides identifying the content-area domain of the measure, the ROMR includes additional information to help users select appropriate measures to meet their needs, such as

- type of staff who can administer the measure
- whether or not the measure has been used with a military population
- age group for whom the measure is appropriate (e.g., adults versus children)
- length of a specific measure (number of items)
- method of administration (e.g., questionnaire, interview)
- published information on reliability and validity.

Select Measures for Dual Use by Both Clinicians and Program Evaluators or Researchers

Although the ROMR is primarily intended for use by program evaluators, it does include some measures that can be used both for research purposes and to inform clinical care. The ROMR includes information on available clinical cutoff scores that are recommended for use in the peer-reviewed literature to determine when individuals require clinical services, to inform clinical case planning, or to screen individuals who may be at risk for developing a psychological disorder. Measures with clinical meaning (i.e., those with clinical cutoff scores) may be useful to clinicians providing novel interventions or other services specifically targeting clinical outcomes, as well as to researchers or evaluators who may be working with these clinicians to determine the effectiveness of their services.

Identify Core Outcome Measures for Evaluating Similar Programs

Government agencies, foundations, or others responsible for monitoring a set of programs could use the ROMR to identify and endorse a specific set of measures that are both reliable and valid across a variety of domains. Consistency in tracking core outcomes or indicators is one important step toward being able to compare the effectiveness of different programs in order to determine which approaches are achieving the greatest benefits for the population served. Measures in the ROMR could also be reviewed to identify a set of screening and assessment instruments that could be instituted consistently across primary care and mental health settings.

Determine Need for Additional Development or Validation of Measures with Military Populations

The ROMR contains a broad array of measures that assess psychological health and constructs related to TBI that have been described in the peer-reviewed literature over the past 10 years. Examining the existing measures currently in use by researchers and program evaluators can be helpful in determining areas in need of additional measure development. For example, there are few measures of force readiness currently being used for research or program evaluation, and the reliability and validity of these measures has not been described in the published literature. Similarly, for some domains (e.g., anxiety), few measures have been validated for use in the military population. Further information about the psychometric properties of these measures will be useful in determining their usefulness for these purposes.

Conclusions

The ROMR is a valuable tool that can facilitate the evaluation and monitoring of programs by providing an online searchable database of measures related to psychological health and TBI. To maintain its usefulness, the ROMR will require frequent updating to include emerging measures and to supplement information on the reliability and validity of measures as it is published. Additions may also be considered to expand areas of the ROMR where fewer measures have been identified. These areas include measures of leadership, force readiness, unit cohesion, and family support. Designated DoD organizations with responsibility for assessing the impact of psychological health and TBI programs should consider making provisions to update the database regularly to ensure its continued relevancy.

Existing Measure Repositories

This appendix describes the existing measure repositories or databases that RAND reviewed when identifying the key features and functions that should be included in the ROMR. These brief descriptions feature the number and types of measures in each repository, as well as the type of information that each repository includes about each measure.

ADAI Substance Use Assessment Instrument Library (2011)

The Alcohol and Drug Abuse Institute (ADAI) at the University of Washington has a free, online database of 750 measures related to the screening and assessment of substance use and substance use disorders. Available information on each measure includes the measure developer and contact information, a link to the measure, the instrument type and target population, scoring information, and validity/reliability information on the measure (as available). The measures are searchable by the target population, the measure's intended use (self-assessment, outcome evaluation, etc.), and keyword. Veterans are a searchable target population, but there are only seven measures attributed to this population.

Buros Institute of Mental Measurements (2011)

The Buros Institute of Mental Measurements reviews commercially available tests that have psychometric data. A hard copy of the *Mental Measurements Yearbook* costs approximately $200. The Buros Institute also hosts a free, searchable online database of more than 3,500 tests, although only a very limited amount of information is available. Further detail is available by purchasing a $15 Buros review, which is a more detailed report available individually for each of the 3,500 tests. These reviews contain basic information on the measure (including the developer and pricing information), a measure description, technical information on the measure, and Buros Institute commentary. The actual measure itself is not included. The *Yearbook* divides its measures into 18 major categories including behavior assessment, intelligence and general aptitude, neuropsychological, and speech and hearing. No measures related to TBI are included.

Center for Outcome Measurement in Brain Injury (2011)

The Center for Outcome Measurement in Brain Injury is an online resource for individuals needing detailed information and support in using outcome measures related to brain injuries. The website contains 31 measures that are commonly used in the field of brain injury rehabilitation and assessment. Available information on each measure includes a brief description, measure reference, and how to access the measure.

Compendium of Assessment and Research Tools (CART) (2011)

The Compendium of Assessment and Research Tools (CART), supported by the Star Center and W. K. Kellogg Foundation, is an online database of nearly 700 instruments for youth development programs. Use of the database is free; it is searchable by domains and subdomains, such as design and implementation (basic program elements), context (factors that have an indirect effect on implementation), and outcomes (where a change is expected to occur). Available information on each measure includes (as applicable and available for each measure) the target population, year created or modified, instrument type, a short description, a link to the measure itself, and associated constructs. This database does not have measures related to military service members.

ETS Test Collection/Carl C. Brigham Library (2011)

The Educational Testing Service has more than 25,000 items in its database. Measures in the ETS database cover a variety of domains including general health and well-being, and educational and career achievement. The information in the database is designed for use by researchers, graduate students, and teachers. There are no specific references to a military population. More than 1,000 tests are downloadable for a $25 distribution fee (abstracts can be viewed free). As of February 2, 2011, 38 of these measures were related to PTSD (of which 7 items were related to "combat"), and 14 measures were related to TBI.

Measuring Violence-Related Attitudes, Behaviors, and Influences Among Youths: A Compendium of Assessment Tools, 2nd ed. (2011)

This compendium published by the Centers for Disease Control, National Center for Injury Prevention and Control, provides researchers and prevention specialists with a free set of tools to assess violence-related beliefs, behaviors, and influences, as well as to evaluate programs to prevent youth violence. There are more than 170 measures intended for use with youths between the ages of 11 and 24 years to assess serious violent and delinquent behavior, conflict resolution strategies, social and emotional competencies, peer influences, parental monitoring and supervision, family relationships, exposure to violence, collective efficacy, and neighborhood characteristics. Available information on each measure includes a brief description, reliability and validity, target population, and the measure developer.

National Center for the Study of PTSD (2011)

The National Center for the Study of PTSD is a federal research and education agency within the Department of Veterans Affairs. It has developed a 52-measure database that is free to use and includes measures relevant to PTSD, including both trauma exposure measures and PTSD screening tools for adults and children. Available information on each measure includes a brief description, sample item, reference, and information about how to obtain the measure.

Patient Reported Outcome and Quality of Life Instruments Database (ProQolid) (2011)

The Patient Reported Outcome and Quality of Life Instruments Database (ProQolid) is an online database of nearly 700 instruments developed by the MAPI Research Institute. The database has two levels: free and advanced (for a fee). The free level offers 14 data fields of information on an instrument including purpose, population, and some basic characteristics (such as the type of instrument). The advanced level contains psychometric properties of measures, methodology of instrument development, and the final version of the measure; access costs a minimum of $750. The measure domains are related more to physical ailments than to mental health, although there are measures related to psychiatry and psychology, which include anxiety and depression measures. Military service members are not a specific population targeted by this database.

Detailed Literature Search Strategies Used to Identify Measures

Table B.1

Database	Domain	Limits	Search Concepts	Results
Military Psychology	Depression, anxiety, PTSD, resilience, and suicide	2008 to current	Concept 1: depression OR anxiety OR posttraumatic stress OR PTSD OR resilience OR suicide OR suicidal AND Concept 2: measure OR inventory OR scale OR assessment OR psychometrics OR questionnaire OR screening OR survey OR checklist OR test AND Concept 3: journal title: Military Psychology	54 total, 1 duplicate, 2 possibly relevant
Military Psychology	TBI	2008 to current	Concept 1: traumatic brain injury AND Concept 2: survey OR instrument OR questionnaire OR scale OR measure OR psychometrics OR screening OR test OR span OR retention OR psychomotor OR sociometric OR checklist AND Concept 3: journal title: Military Psychology	6 total, 4 duplicates, none relevant
PsycINFO	Depression, anxiety, PTSD, resilience, and suicide	English, published in 2000 to current, peer-reviewed journal articles only	Concept 1: attitude measure* OR inventory OR inventories OR multidimensional scaling OR psychiatric evaluation OR psychological assessments OR psychometrics OR questionnaires OR rating scales OR screening OR statistical measurement OR subtests OR surveys OR symptom checklists OR testing AND Concept 2: posttraumatic stress disorder OR DE "acute stress disorder" or DE "death anxiety" or DE "generalized anxiety disorder" or DE "obsessive compulsive disorder" or DE "panic disorder" or DE "phobias" or TI anxiety OR DE "dysthymic disorder" or DE "endogenous depression" or DE "reactive depression" or DE "recurrent depression" or DE "treatment resistant depression" OR TI depression OR resilience OR suicid* AND Concept 3: TI valid* OR DE valid* OR TI reliab* OR DE reliab*	790 total; after deleting duplicates, 309 unique results, with 95 judged possibly relevant

Table B.1—Continued

Database	Domain	Limits	Search Concepts	Results
PubMed	Anxiety, depression, and PTSD	Humans, English, published in 2000 to current	Concept 1: posttraumatic stress disorder* OR depressive disorder[TI] OR depression[MeSH Terms] OR depression[TI] OR anxiety[MeSH Terms] OR anxiety[TI] OR depressive disorder, major[MeSH] OR dysthymic disorder[Mesh] AND Concept 2: survey OR surveys OR instrument OR instruments OR questionnaire OR questionnaires OR psychiatric status rating scales OR measure[tiab] OR measures[tiab] OR psychiatric status rating scales OR psychometrics AND Concept 3: validation studies as topic[Mesh] OR valid*[ti] OR reliab*[ti] NOT Concept 4: postpartum OR post-partum OR post-natal OR postnatal NOT Concept 5: editorial OR letter OR comment	829 total, with 257 judged possibly relevant
PILOTS	All	English, published in 2000 to current, peer-reviewed journal articles only	Concept 1: survey OR surveys OR instrument OR instruments OR questionnaire OR questionnaires OR psychiatric status rating scales OR measure OR measures OR psychiatric status rating scales OR psychometrics AND Concept 2: valid* OR reliab*	674 total; after deleting duplicates, 601 unique results, with 141 results judged possibly relevant
PsycINFO	TBI	English, published in 2000 to current, peer-reviewed journal articles only	Concept 1: aptitude measure* OR attitude measure* OR comprehension test* OR digit span test* OR intelligence measure* OR inventory OR inventories OR multidimensional scaling OR perceptual measure* OR psychiatric evaluation OR psychological assessments OR psychometrics OR questionnaires OR rating scales OR retention measures OR screening OR sensorimotor measures OR sociometric test* OR speech and hearing measures OR statistical measurement OR subtests OR survey* OR symptom checklist* OR testing OR verbal test* AND Concept 2: traumatic brain injur* AND Concept 3: TI valid* OR DE valid* OR TI reliab* OR DE reliab*	116 total; after deleting duplicates, 94 unique results, with 76 judged possibly relevant
PubMed	TBI	Humans, English, published in 2000 to current	Concept 1: traumatic brain injury AND Concept 2: survey OR surveys OR instrument OR instruments OR questionnaire OR questionnaires OR psychiatric status rating scales OR measure[tiab] OR measures[tiab] OR psychiatric status rating scales OR psychometrics OR aptitude tests OR digit span OR language tests OR hearing tests OR neuropsychological tests OR retention [MeSH] OR psychomotor performance OR sociometric techniques OR speech production measurement AND Concept 3: "validation studies as topic"[MeSH] OR valid*[tiab] OR reliab*[tiab] NOT Concept 4: editorial OR letter OR comment	89 total, 1 duplicate, with 64 unique results judged possibly relevant

Table B.1—Continued

Database	Domain	Limits	Search Concepts	Results
PubMed	Resilience and suicidal thoughts	Humans, English, published in 2000 to current	Concept 1: resilienc* OR suicid* AND Concept 2: survey OR surveys OR instrument OR instruments OR questionnaire OR questionnaires OR psychiatric status rating scales OR measure[tiab] OR measures[tiab] OR psychiatric status rating scales OR psychometrics AND Concept 3: "validation studies as topic"[MeSH] OR valid*[ti] OR reliab*[ti] NOT Concept 4: editorial OR letter OR comment	94 total; after deleting duplicates, 73 unique results, with 14 judged possibly relevant
PILOTS	Military measures	English, published in 2000 to current, peer-reviewed journal articles only	Concept 1: survey OR surveys OR instrument OR instruments OR questionnaire OR questionnaires OR psychiatric status rating scales OR measure OR measures OR psychiatric status rating scales OR psychometrics AND Concept 2: valid* OR reliab* AND military measures concepts: military AND readiness, "unit cohesion," "force preservation," military AND (confidence OR trust OR perception* OR support*) AND (leader* OR unit)	1 total
PsycINFO	Military measures	English, published in 2000 to current, peer-reviewed journal articles only	Concept 1: attitude measure* OR inventory OR inventories OR multidimensional scaling OR psychiatric evaluation OR psychological assessments OR psychometrics OR questionnaires OR rating scales OR screening OR statistical measurement OR subtests OR surveys OR symptom checklists OR testing AND Concept 2: valid* OR reliab* AND military measures concepts: military AND readiness, "unit cohesion," "force preservation," military AND (confidence OR trust OR perception* OR support*) AND (leader* OR unit)	17 total, 5 duplicates
PubMed	Military measures	Humans, English, published in 2000 to current	Concept 1: survey OR surveys OR instrument OR instruments OR questionnaire OR questionnaires OR psychiatric status rating scales OR measure[tiab] OR measures[tiab] OR psychiatric status rating scales OR psychometrics AND Concept 2: "validation studies as topic"[MeSH] OR valid*[tiab] OR reliab*[tiab] AND military measures concepts: military AND readiness, "unit cohesion," "force preservation," military AND (confidence OR trust OR perception* OR support*) AND (leader* OR unit)	23 total, 2 duplicates

References Included in the RAND Online Measure Repository

Abraido-Lanza AF, Guier C, Colon RM. "Psychological Thriving Among Latinas with Chronic Illness." *Journal of Social Issues*, 1998, 54: 405–424.

Abramson LY, Metalsky GI. "The Cognitive Style Questionnaire: Measurement of Negative Cognitive Styles About Self and Consequences." Unpublished manuscript, University of Wisconsin–Madison, 1989.

Amdur RL, Liberzon I. "The Structure of Posttraumatic Stress Disorder Symptoms in Combat Veterans: A Confirmatory Factor Analysis of the Impact of Event Scale." *Journal of Anxiety Disorders*, 2001, 15 (4): 345–357.

Angold A, Costello EJ, Messer SC, Pickles A, Winder F, Silver D. "The Development of a Short Questionnaire for Use in Epidemiological Studies of Depression in Children and Adolescents." *International Journal of Methods in Psychiatric Research*, 2005, 5: 237–249.

Ayvasik HB, Tutarel-Kislak S. "Factor Structure and Reliability of the Anxiety Sensitivity Profile in a Turkish Sample." *European Journal of Psychological Assessment*, 2004, 20: 358–367.

Aziz AM, Kenford S. "Comparability of Telephone and Face-to-Face Interviews in Assessing Patients with Posttraumatic Stress Disorder." *Journal of Psychiatric Practice*, 2004, 10 (5): 307–313.

Bagby RM, Ryder AG, Deborah R, Schuller MD, Marshall MB. "The Hamilton Depression Rating Scale: Has the Gold Standard Become a Lead Weight?" *American Journal of Psychiatry*, 2004, 161: 2163–2177.

Barnett MD, Ledoux T, Garcini LM, Baker J. "Type D Personality and Chronic Pain: Construct and Concurrent Validity of the DS14." *Journal of Clinical Psychology in Medical Settings*, 2009, 16 (2): 194–199.

Barrett D. "Cognitive Functioning and Posttraumatic Stress Disorder." *American Journal of Psychiatry*, 1996, 153: 1492–1494.

Bartone PT. "Test-Retest Reliability of the Dispositional Resilience Scale-15, A Brief Hardiness Scale." *Psychological Reports*, 2007, 101: 943–944.

Bartone PT, Ursano AR, Wright K, Ingraham L. "The Impact of a Military Air Disaster on the Health of Assistance Workers: A Prospective Study." *Journal of Nervous and Mental Disease*, 1989, 177: 317–328.

Beck A, Wiessman A, Lester D, Trexler L. "The Measurement of Pessimism: The Hopelessness Scale." *Journal of Counseling and Clinical Psychology*, 1974, 42 (6): 142–144.

Beck AT, Epstein N, Brown G, Steer G, Steer RA. "An Inventory for Measuring Clinical Anxiety: Psychometric Properties." *Journal of Consulting and Clinical Psychology*, 1988, 56: 893–897.

Beck AT, Steer RA, Ranieri WF. "Scale for Suicide Ideation: Psychometric Properties of a Self-Report Version." *Journal of Clinical Psychology*, 1988, 44 (4): 215–227.

Beidel DC, Turner SM, Morris TL. "A New Inventory to Assess Childhood Social Anxiety and Phobia: The Social Phobia and Anxiety Inventory for Children." *Psychological Assessment*, 1995, 7: 73–79.

Bernstein DP, Fink L. *Childhood Trauma Questionnaire: A Retrospective Self-Report Manual.* San Antonio, TX: The Psychological Corporation, 1998.

Betemps E, Baker DG. "Evaluation of the Mississippi PTSD Scale—Revised Using Rasch Measurement." *Mental Health Services Research*, 2004, 6 (2): 117–125.

Birmaher B, Khetarpal S, Brent D, Cully M, et al. "The Screen for Child Anxiety Related Emotional Disorders (SCARED): Scale Construction and Psychometric Characteristics." *Journal of the American Academy of Child and Adolescent Psychiatry*, 1997, 36: 545–553.

Blais AR, Thompson MM, McCreary DR. "The Development and Validation of the Army Post-Deployment Reintegration Scale." *Military Psychology*, 2009, 21 (3): 365–386.

Blake DD, Weathers FW, Nagy LM, Kaloupek DG, et al. "The Development of a Clinician-Administered PTSD Scale." *Journal of Traumatic Stress*, 1995, 8: 75–90.

Blanchard EB, Jones-Alexander J, Buckley TC, Forneris CA. "Psychometric Properties of the PTSD Checklist (PCL)." *Behaviour Research and Therapy*, 1996, 34 (8): 669–673.

Bliese PD, Wright KM, Adler AB, Cabrera O, Castrol CA, Hoge CW. "Validating the Primary Care Posttraumatic Stress Disorder Screen and the Posttraumatic Stress Disorder Checklist with Soldiers Returning from Combat." *Journal of Consulting and Clinical Psychology*, 2008, 76: 272–281.

Bobić J, Pavićević L, Drenovac M. "Some Psychological Consequences of War Imprisonment." *Studia Psychologica*, 1997, 39 (1): 45–51. Available from PsycINFO.

Boisvert JA, McCreary DR, Wright KD, Asmundson GJ. "Factorial Validity of the Center for Epidemiologic Studies-Depression (CES-D) Scale in Military Peacekeepers." *Depression and Anxiety*, 2003, 17 (1): 19–25.

Bowden S, Saklofske D, Weiss L. "Augmenting the Core Battery with Supplementary Subtests: Wechsler Adult Intelligence Scale—IV Measurement Invariance Across the United States and Canada." *Assessment*, 2011, 18 (2): 133–140.

Brener ND, Kann L, McManus T, Kinchen SA, Sundberg EC, Ross JG. "Reliability of the 1999 Youth Risk Behavior Survey Questionnaire." *Journal of Adolescent Health*, 2002, 31: 336–342.

Breslau N, Peterson EL, Kessler RC, Schultz LR. "Short Screening Scale for DSM-IV Posttraumatic Stress Disorder." *American Journal of Psychiatry*, 1999, 156: 908–911.

Briere J. *The Trauma Symptom Inventory Professional Manual.* Odessa, FL: Psychological Assessment Resources, 1995.

Britt TW. "The Stigma of Psychological Problems in a Work Environment: Evidence from the Screening of Service Members Returning from Bosnia." *Journal of Applied Social Psychology*, 2000, 30: 1599–1618.

Britt TW, Greene-Shortridge TM, Brink S. "Perceived Stigma and Barriers to Care for Psychological Treatment: Implications for Reactions to Stressors in Different Contexts." *Journal of Social and Clinical Psychology*, 2008, 27: 317–335.

Britt TW, Greene TM, Castro CA, Hoge CW. "The Stigma of Psychological Problems in the Military." Paper presented at: APA/NIOSH Work, Stress, and Health Conference; March 3, 2006; Miami, FL.

Brunet A, Weiss DS, Metzler TJ, Best SR, Neylan TC, Rogers C, Fagan J, Marmar CR. "The Peritraumatic Distress Inventory: A Proposed Measure of PTSD Criterion A2." *American Journal of Psychiatry*, 2001, 158 (9): 1480–1485.

Bush BA, Novack TA, Schneider JJ, Madan A. "Depression Following Traumatic Brain Injury: The Validity of the CES-D as a Brief Screening Device," *Journal of Clinical Psychology in Medical Settings*, 2004, 11 (3): 195–201.

Butcher JN, Dahlstrom WG, Graham JR, Tellegen A, Kaemmer B. *MMPI-2 (Minnesota Multiphasic Personality Inventory-2): Manual for Administration and Scoring.* Minneapolis: University of Minnesota Press, 1989.

Buysse DJ, Reynolds CF, Monk TH, Berman SR, Kupfer DJ. "The Pittsburgh Sleep Quality Index: A New Instrument for Psychiatric Practice and Research." *Psychiatry Research*, 1989, 28: 193–213.

Calhoun PS, Earnst KS, Tucker DD, Kirby AC, Beckham JC. "Feigning Combat-Related Posttraumatic Stress Disorder on the Personality Assessment Inventory." *Journal of Personality Assessment*, 2000, 75 (2): 338–350.

Calhoun PS, McDonald SD, Guerra VS, Eggleston AM, Beckham JC, Straits-Troster K. "Clinical Utility of the Primary Care–PTSD Screen Among U.S. Veterans Who Served Since September 11, 2001." *Psychiatry Research*, 2010, 178: 330–335.

Campbell-Sills L, Stein MB. "Psychometric Analysis and Refinement of the Connor-Davidson Resilience Scale (CD-RISC): Validation of a 10-item Measure of Resilience." *Journal of Traumatic Stress*, 2007, 20 (6): 1019–1028.

Carlozzi NE, Long PJ. "Reliability and Validity of the SCL-90-R PTSD Subscale." *Journal of Interpersonal Violence*, 2008, 23 (9): 1162–1176.

Carlson EB. "Psychometric Study of a Brief Screen for PTSD: Assessing the Impact of Multiple Traumatic Events." *Assessment*, 2001, 8 (4): 431–441.

Chang LC, Frost LZ, Chao S. "Instrument Development with Web Surveys and Multiple Imputations." *Military Psychology*, 2010, 22: 7–23.

Chorpita BF, Moffitt CF, Gray J. "Psychometric Properties of the Revised Child Anxiety and Depression Scale in a Clinical Sample." *Behaviour Research and Therapy*, 2005, 43 (3): 309–322.

Chorpita BF, Yim L, Moffitt CE, Umemoto LA, Francis SE. "Assessment of Symptoms of DSM-IV Anxiety and Depression in Children: A Revised Child Anxiety and Depression Scale." *Behaviour Research and Therapy*, 2000, 38: 835–855.

Clark DB, Donovan JE. "Reliability and Validity of the Hamilton Anxiety Rating Scale in an Adolescent Sample." *Journal of the American Academy of Child and Adolescent Psychiatry*, 1994, 33: 354–360.

Collins KA, Westra HA, Dozois DJA, Stewart SH. "The Validity of the Brief Version of the Fear of Negative Evaluation Scale." *Anxiety Disorders*, 2005, 19: 345–359.

Connor KM, Davidson JR. "Assessment of Resilience in the Aftermath of Trauma." *Journal of Clinical Psychiatry*, 2006, 67, Supplement 2: 46–49.

Connor KM, Davidson JR. "Development of a New Resilience Scale: The Connor-Davidson Resilience Scale (CD-RISC)." *Depression and Anxiety*, 2003, 18: 76–82.

Cook JM, Elhai JD, Cassidy EL, Ruzek JI, Ram GD, Sheikh JI. "Assessment of Trauma Exposure and Post-Traumatic Stress in Long Term Care Veterans: Preliminary Data on Psychometrics and Post-Traumatic Stress Disorder Prevalence." *Military Medicine*, 2005, 170 (10): 862–866.

Corson K, Gerrity MS, Dobscha SK. "Screening for Depression and Suicidality in a VA Primary Care Setting: 2 Items Are Better Than 1 Item." *American Journal of Managed Care*, 2000, 10 (11): 839–845.

Costello EJ, Angold A. "Scales to Assess Child and Adolescent Depression: Checklists, Screens, and Nets." *Journal of the American Academy of Child and Adolescent Psychiatry*, 2006, 27: 726–737.

Craft LL. "Exercise and Clinical Depression: Examining Two Psychological Mechanisms." *Psychology of Sport and Exercise*, 2005, 6: 151–171.

Crandall M, Lammers C, Senders C, Savedra M, Braun JV. "Initial Validation of a Numeric Zero to Ten Scale to Measure Children's State Anxiety." *Anesthesia & Analgesia*, 2007, 105: 1250–1253.

Crawford EF, Lang AJ, Laffaye C. "An Evaluation of the Psychometric Properties of the Traumatic Events Questionnaire in Primary Care Patients." *Journal of Traumatic Stress*, 2008, 21 (1): 109–112.

Davidson JRT, Book SW, Colket JT, Tupler LA, et al. "Assessment of a New Self-Rating Scale for Posttraumatic Stress Disorder." *Psychological Medicine*, 1997, 27: 153–160.

Daviss WB, Birmaher B, Melhem NA, Axelson DA, Michaels SM, Brent DA. "Criterion Validity of the Mood and Feelings Questionnaire for Depressive Episodes in Clinic and Non-Clinic Subjects." *Journal of Child Psychology and Psychiatry*, 2006, 47 (10): 927–934.

Daviss WB, Burleson B, Melhem NA, Axelson DA, Michaels SA, Brent DA. "Criterion Validity of the Mood and Feelings Questionnaire for Depressive Episodes in Clinic and Non-Clinic Subjects." *Journal of Child Psychology and Psychiatry*, 2006, 47 (9): 927–934.

Deans C, Byrne DG. "A Scale to Measure Non-Traumatic Military Operational Stress." *Stress and Health*, 2006, 23: 53–62.

Denollet J. "DS14: Standard Assessment of Negative Affectivity, Social Inhibition, and Type D Personality." *Psychosomatic Medicine*, 2005, 67: 89–90.

Dobreva-Martinova T. *Psychometric Analysis of the Stress in the Military Service Based on Surveys of Deployed Canadian Forces Personnel* (Sponsor Research Report 98-16). Ottawa, Ontario: Department of National Defence, Directorate for Human Resource Research and Evaluation, 1998.

Dremsa TL. "Pilot Testing the Readiness Estimate and Deployability Index Revised for Air Force Nurses." *Military Medicine*, 2004, 169 (1): 12–16.

Dremsa TL, Ryan-Wenger NA, Reineck C. "Reliability and Validity Testing of a Short Form of the Readiness Estimate and Deployability Index Revised for Air Force Nurses." *Military Medicine*, 2006, 171 (9): 879–884.

Ebell MH. "Screening Instruments for Depression." *American Family Physician*, 2008, 78 (2): 244–246.

Eisen SV. "Behavior and Symptom Identification Scale (BASIS-32)." In *Outcomes Assessment in Clinical Practice*. LI Sederer and B Dickey (eds.). Baltimore, MD: Williams & Wilkins, 1996, pp. 65–69.

Eisen SV, Wilcox M, Leff HS, Schaefer E, Culhane MA. "Assessing Behavioral Health Outcomes in Outpatient Programs: Reliability and Validity of BASIS-32." *Journal of Behavioral Health Services and Research*, 1999, 26 (1): 5–17.

Elhai JD, Franklin CL, Gray MJ. "The SCID PTSD Module's Trauma Screen: Validity with Two Samples in Detecting Trauma History." *Depression and Anxiety*, 2008, 25 (9): 737–741.

Elhai JD, Gold PB, Frueh BC, Gold SN. "Cross-Validation of the MMPI-2 in Detecting Malingered Posttraumatic Stress Disorder." *Journal of Personality Assessment*, 2000, 75 (3): 449–463.

Elhai JD, Gray MJ, Naifeh JA, Butcher JJ, et al. "Utility of the Trauma Symptom Inventory's Atypical Response Scale in Detecting Malingered Post-Traumatic Stress Disorder." *Assessment*, 2005, 12 (2): 210.

Elhai JD, Naifeh JA, Zucker IS, Gold SN, Deitsch SE, Frueh BC. "Discriminating Malingered from Genuine Civilian Posttraumatic Stress Disorder: A Validation of Three MMPI-2 Infrequency Scales (F, FP, and FPTSD)." *Assessment*, 2004, 11 (2): 139–144.

Endicott J, Nee J, Yang R, Wohlberg C. "Pediatric Quality of Life Enjoyment and Satisfaction Questionnaire (PQ-LES-Q): Reliability and Validity." *Journal of the American Academy of Child & Adolescent Psychiatry*, 2006, 45 (4): 401–407.

Endicott JE, Spitzer RL, Fleiss JL, Cohen J. "The Global Assessment Scale: A Procedure for Measuring the Overall Severity of Psychiatric Disturbance." *Archives of General Psychology*, 1976, 33 (6): 766–771.

Erlanger D, Feldman K, Kutner T, Kaushik H, et al. "Development and Validation of a Web-Based Neuropsychological Test Protocol for Sports-Related Return-to-Play Decision-Making." *Archives of Clinical Neuropsychology*, 2003, 18 (3): 293–316.

Erlanger DM, Kaushik T, Broshek D, Freeman J, Feldman D, Festa J. "Development and Validation of a Web-Based Screening Tool for Monitoring Cognitive Status." *Journal of Head Trauma Rehabilitation*, 2002, 17 (5): 458–476.

Fikretoglu D, Brunet A, Poundja J, Guay S, Pedlar D. "Validation of the Deployment Risk and Resilience Inventory in French-Canadian Veterans: Findings on the Relation Between Deployment Experiences and Postdeployment Health." *Canadian Journal of Psychiatry*, 2006, 51: 755–763.

Findler M, Cantor C, Haddad L, Gordon W, Ashman T. "The Reliability and Validity of the SF-36 Health Survey Questionnaire for Use with Individuals with Traumatic Brain Injury." *Brain Injury*, 2001, 15 (8): 715–723.

First MB, Spitzer RL, Gibbon M, Williams JB. *Structured Clinical Interview for DSM-IV Axis I Disorders, Clinician Version (SCID-CV)*. Washington, DC: American Psychiatric Press, 1996.

Firth KM, Smith K. "A Survey of Multidimensional Health and Fitness." *Military Medicine*, 2010, 175 (8), Supplement 1: 110–117.

Foa EB, Cashman L, Jaycox L, Perry KJ. "The Validation of a Self-Report Measure of Posttraumatic Stress Disorder: The Posttraumatic Diagnostic Scale." *Psychological Assessment*, 1997, 9: 445–451.

Foa EB, Riggs DS, Dancu CV, Rothbaum BO. "Reliability and Validity of a Brief Instrument for Assessing Posttraumatic Stress Disorder." *Journal of Traumatic Stress*, 1993, 6: 459–473.

Foa EB, Tolin DF. "Comparison of the PTSD Symptom Scale-Interview Version and the Clinician-Administered PTSD Scale." *Journal of Traumatic Stress*, 2000, 13 (2): 181–191.

Ford JD, Kidd P. "Early Childhood Trauma and Disorders of Extreme Stress as Predictors of Treatment Outcome with Chronic PTSD." *Journal of Traumatic Stress*, 1998, 11: 743–761.

Foy DW, Sipprelle RC, Rueger DB, Carroll EM. "Etiology of Posttraumatic Stress Disorder in Vietnam Veterans: Analysis of Premilitary, Military, and Combat Exposure Influences." *Journal of Consulting and Clinical Psychology*, 1994, 1: 181–192.

Franklin CL, Sheeran T, Zimmerman M. "Screening for Trauma Histories, Posttraumatic Stress Disorder (PTSD), and Subthreshold PTSD in Psychiatric Outpatients." *Psychological Assessment*, 2002, 14 (4): 467–471.

Frueh BC, Gold PB, Dammeyer M, Pellegrin KL, et al. "Differentiation of Depression and PTSD Symptoms in Combat Veterans." *Depression and Anxiety*, 2000, 11 (4): 175–179.

Gade PA, Tiggle RB, Schumm WR. "The Measurement and Consequences of Military Organizational Commitment in Soldiers and Spouses." *Military Psychology*, 2003, 15: 191–207.

Gamez W, Kotov R, Watson D. "The Validity of Self-Report Assessment of Avoidance and Distress." *Anxiety Stress & Coping*, 2010, 23 (1): 87–99.

Gaynes BN, DeVeaugh-Geiss J, Weir S, Gu H, et al. "Feasibility and Diagnostic Validity of the M-3 Checklist: A Brief, Self-Rated Screen for Depressive, Bipolar, Anxiety, and Post-Traumatic Stress Disorders in Primary Care." *Annals of Family Medicine*, 2010, 8 (2): 160–169.

Germain A, Hall M, Krakow B, Shear MK, Buysse DJ. "A Brief Sleep Scale for Posttraumatic Stress Disorder: Pittsburgh Sleep Quality Index Addendum for PTSD." *Journal of Anxiety Disorders*, 2005, 19 (2): 233–244.

Giannopoulou I, Smith P, Ecker C, Strouthos M, Dikaiakou A, Yule W. "Factor Structure of the Children's Revised Impact of Event Scale (CRIES) with Children Exposed to Earthquake." *Personality and Individual Differences*, 2006, 40: 1027–1037.

Gibbons RD, Rush AJ, Immekus JC. "On the Psychometric Validity of the Domains of the PDSQ: An Illustration of the Bi-Factor Item Response Theory Model." *Journal of Psychiatric Research*, 2009, 43 (4): 401–410.

Gonzalez JM, Bowden CL, Katz MM, Thompson P, et al. "Development of the Bipolar Inventory of Symptoms Scale: Concurrent Validity, Discriminant Validity and Retest Reliability." *International Journal of Methods in Psychiatric Research*, 2008, 17 (4): 198–209.

Gouvier WD, Blanton PD, LaPorte KK, et al. "Reliability and Validity of the Disability Rating Scale and the Levels of Cognitive Functioning Scale in Monitoring Recovery from Severe Head Injury." *Archives of Physical Medicine and Rehabilitation*, 1987, 68: 94–97.

Gray MJ, Elhai JD, Briere JN. "Evaluation of the Atypical Response Scale of the Trauma Symptom Inventory–2 in Detecting Simulated Posttraumatic Stress Disorder." *Journal of Anxiety Disorders*, 2010, 24 (5): 447–451.

Gualtieri CT. "An Internet-Based Symptom Questionnaire That Is Reliable, Valid, and Available to Psychiatrists, Neurologists, and Psychologists." *Medscape General Medicine*, 2007, 9 (4): 3.

Gualtieri CT, Johnson LG. "A Computerized Test Battery Sensitive to Mild and Severe Brain Injury." *Medscape Journal of Medicine*, 2008, 10 (4): 90.

Gualtieri CT, Johnson LG. "Reliability and Validity of a Computerized Neurocognitive Test Battery, CNS Vital Signs." *Archives of Clinical Neuropsychology*, 2006, 21 (7): 623–643.

Gutierrez PM. "Self-Harm Behavior Questionnaire (SHBQ)." Unpublished manuscript, Northern Illinois University, 2008.

Gutierrez PM, Osman A, Barrios FX, Kopper BA. "Development and Initial Validation of the Self-Harm Behavior Questionnaire." *Journal of Personality Assessment*, 2001, 77 (3): 475–490.

Haeffel GJ, Gibb BE, Metalsky GI, Alloy LB, et al. "Measuring Cognitive Vulnerability to Depression: Development and Validation of the Cognitive Style Questionnaire." *Clinical Psychology Review*, 2008, 28 (5): 824–836.

Hamilton M. "An Assessment of Anxiety States by Rating." *British Journal of Medical Psychology*, 1959, 32 (1): 50–55.

Hammarberg M. "Penn Inventory for Posttraumatic Stress Disorder: Psychometric Properties." *Psychological Assessment*, 1999, 4 (1): 67–76.

Hankin BL, Abramson LY. "Measuring Cognitive Vulnerability to Depression in Adolescence: Reliability, Validity, and Gender Differences." *Journal of Clinical Child and Adolescent Psychology*, 2002, 31 (4): 491–504.

Hart T, Whyte J, Ellis C, Chervoneva I. "Construct Validity of an Attention Rating Scale for Traumatic Brain Injury." *Neuropsychology*, 2009, 23 (6): 729–735.

Hays RD, Sherbourne CD, Mazel RM. "The RAND 36-Item Health Survey 1.0." *Health Economics*, 1993, 2: 217–227.

Heimberg RG, Holaway RM. "Examination of the Known-Groups Validity of the Liebowitz Social Anxiety Scale." *Depression and Anxiety*, 2007, 24: 447–454.

Heimberg RG, Horner KJ, Juster HR, Safren SA, et al. "Psychometric Properties of the Liebowitz Social Anxiety Scale." *Psychological Medicine*, 1999, 29: 199–212.

Hellerstein DJ, Batchelder ST, Lee A, Borisovskaya M. "Rating Dysthymia: An Assessment of the Construct and Content Validity of the Cornell Dysthymia Rating Scale." *Journal of Affective Disorders*, 2002, 71: 85–96.

Heubeck BG, Neill JT. "Internal Validity and Reliability of the 30 Item Mental Health Inventory for Australian Adolescents." *Psychological Reports*, 2000, 87: 431–440.

Hoelzle J, Nelson N, Smith C. "Comparison of Wechsler Memory Scale–Fourth Edition (WMS–IV) and Third Edition (WMS–III) Dimensional Structures: Improved Ability to Evaluate Auditory and Visual Constructs." *Journal of Clinical and Experimental Neuropsychology*, 2011, 33 (3): 283–291.

Hoge CW, Castro CA, Messer SC, McGurk D, Cotting D, Koffman RL. "Combat Duty in Iraq and Afghanistan, Mental Health Problems, and Barriers to Care." *New England Journal of Medicine*, 2004, 351: 13–22.

Hoge CW, Engel Jr. CC, Orman DT, Crandell EO, et al. "Development of a Brief Questionnaire to Measure Mental Health Outcomes Among Pentagon Employees Following the September 11, 2001 Attack." *Military Medicine*, 2002, 167, Supplement 9: 60–63.

Horowitz M, Wilner N, Alvarez W. "Impact of Event Scale: A Measure of Subjective Stress." *Psychosomatic Medicine*, 1979, 41: 209–218. As of October 19, 2011:
http://www.armymedicine.army.mil/reports/mhat/mhat/annex_a.pdf
http://www.armymedicine.army.mil/reports/mhat/mhat_vi/MHAT_VI-OIF_Redacted.pdf

Houskamp BM, Foy DW. "The Assessment of Posttraumatic Stress Disorder in Battered Women." *Journal of Interpersonal Violence*, 1991, 6: 368–376.

Hoyt DR, Creech JC. "The Life Satisfaction Index: A Methodological and Theoretical Critique." *Journal of Gerontology*, 1983, 38: 111–116.

Iannuzzo RW, Jaeger J, Goldberg JF, Kafantaris V, Sublette ME. "Development and Reliability of the Ham-D/MADRS Interview: An Integrated Depression Symptom Rating Scale." *Psychiatry Research*, 2006, 145 (1): 21–37.

Inderbitzen-Nolan H, Davies CA, McKeon ND. "Investigating the Construct Validity of the SPAI-C: Comparing the Sensitivity and Specificity of the SPAI-C and the SAS-A." *Journal of Anxiety Disorders*, 2004, 18 (4): 547–560.

Inderbitzen-Nolan HM, Walters KS. "Social Anxiety Scale for Adolescents: Normative Data and Further Evidence of Construct Validity." *Journal of Clinical Child Psychology*, 2000, 29 (3): 360–371.

Iqbal SU, Rogers W, Selim A, Qian S, et al. "The Veterans RAND 12 Item Health Survey (VR-12): What Is It and How It Is Used–2009." *Quality of Life Research*, 2009, 18: 43–52.

Jay M, John OP. "A Depressive Symptom Scale for the California Psychological Inventory: Construct Validation of the CPI-D." *Psychological Assessment*, 2004, 16 (3): 299–309.

Jones D, Kazis L, Lee A, Rogers W, et al. "Health Status Assessments Using the Veterans SF-12 and SF-36: Methods for Evaluating Outcomes in the Veterans Health Administration." *Journal of Ambulatory Care Management*, 2001, 24 (3), 68–86.

Jordan NN, Hoge CW, Tobler SK, Wells J, Dydek GJ, Egerton WE. "Mental Health Impact of 9/11 Pentagon Attack: Validation of a Rapid Assessment Tool." *American Journal of Preventive Medicine*, 2004, 26 (4): 284–293.

Joseph S, Williams R, Yule W. "Changes in Outlook Following Disaster: Preliminary Development of a Measure to Assess Positive and Negative Responses." *Journal of Traumatic Stress*, 1993, 6: 271–279.

Joseph SP, Linley A, Andrews L, Harris G, et al. "Assessing Positive and Negative Changes in the Aftermath of Adversity: Psychometric Evaluation of the Changes in Outlook Questionnaire." *Psychological Assessment*, 2005, 17 (1): 70–80.

Joseph SP, Linley A, Shevlin M, Goodfellow B, Butler LB. "Assessing Positive and Negative Changes in the Aftermath of Adversity: A Short Form of the Changes in Outlook Questionnaire." *Journal of Loss and Trauma*, 2006, 11: 85–99.

Kassam-Adams N. "The Acute Stress Checklist for Children (ASC-Kids): Development of a Child Self-Report Measure." *Journal of Traumatic Stress*, 2006, 19 (1): 129–139.

Katz LS, Cojucar G, Davenport CT, Pedram C, Lindl C. "Post-Deployment Readjustment Inventory: Reliability, Validity, and Gender Differences." *Military Psychology*, 2010, 22 (1): 41–56.

Kazis LE, Miller DR, Skinner KM, Lee A, et al. "Patient-Reported Measures of Health: The Veterans Health Study." *Journal of Ambulatory Care Management*, 2004, 27 (1): 70–83.

Kazis LE, Selim A, Rogers WH, Ren XS, Lee A, Miller DR. "Dissemination of Methods and Results from the Veterans Health Study: Final Comments and Implications for Future Monitoring Strategies Within and Outside the Veterans Healthcare System." *Journal of Ambulatory Care Management*, 2006, 29: 310–319.

Kazis LE, Selim A, Rogers WH, Ren XS, Lee A, Miller DR. "Veterans RAND 12 Item Health Survey (VR-12): A White Paper Summary." As of October 18, 2011: http://www.hosonline.org/surveys/hos/download/Veterans_RAND_12_Item_Health_Survey_White_Paper_Summary.pdf

Keane TM, Caddell JM, Taylor KL. "Mississippi Scale for Combat-Related Posttraumatic Stress Disorder: Three Studies in Reliability and Validity." *Journal of Consulting and Clinical Psychology*, 1988, 56 (1): 85–90.

Keane TM, Fairbank JA, Caddell JM, Zimering RT, Taylor KL, Mora CA. "Clinical Evaluation of a Measure to Assess Combat Exposure." *Psychological Assessment*, 1989, 1: 53–55.

Kimerling RE, Ouimette PC, Prins A, Nisco P, et al. "Brief Report: Utility of a Short Screening Scale for DSM-IV PTSD in Primary Care." *Journal of General Internal Medicine*, 2006, 21 (1): 65–67.

King L, Vogt D, Knight J, Samper R. "Deployment Risk and Resilience Inventory: A Collection of Measures for Studying Deployment-Related Experiences of Military Personnel and Veterans." *Military Psychology*, 2006, 18 (2): 89–120.

King LA, King DW, Leskin G, Foy DW. "The Los Angeles Symptom Checklist: A Self-Report Measure of Posttraumatic Stress Disorder." *Assessment*, 1995, 2 (1): 1–17.

Kroenke K, Spitzer RL, Williams JBW. "The PHQ-9: Validity of a Brief Depression Severity Measure." *Journal of General Internal Medicine*, 2001, 16: 606–613.

Kroenke K, Strine TW, Spitzer RL, Williams JBW, Berry JT, Mokdad AH. "The PHQ-8 as a Measure of Current Depression in the General Population." *Journal of Affective Disorders*, 2009, 114: 163–173.

Kroenke KR, Spitzer RL, Williams JB. "The Patient Health Questionnaire-2: Validity of a Two-Item Depression Screener." *Medical Care*, 2003, 41 (11): 1284–1292.

Kronenberger WG, Causey D, Carter BD. "Validity of the Pediatric Inpatient Behavior Scale in an Inpatient Psychiatric Setting." *Journal of Clinical Psychology*, 2001, 57 (12): 1421–1434.

Kubany ES, Haynes SN, Leisen MB, Owens JA, Kaplan AS, Watson SB, Burns K. "Development and Preliminary Validation of a Brief Broad-Spectrum Measure of Trauma Exposure: The Traumatic Life Events Questionnaire." *Psychological Assessment*, 2000, 12 (2): 210–224.

Laenen A, Alonso A, Molenberghs G, Vangeneugden T, Mallinckrodt CH. "Using Longitudinal Data from a Clinical Trial in Depression to Assess the Reliability of Its Outcome Scales." *Journal of Psychiatric Research*, 2009, 43 (7): 730–738.

Lang AJ, Stein MB. "An Abbreviated PTSD Checklist for Use as a Screening Instrument in Primary Care." *Behaviour Research and Therapy*, 2005, 43 (5): 585–594.

Lauterbach D, Vrana S. "Reliability and Validity of a Self-Report Measure of Posttraumatic Stress Disorder." Poster presented at: Conference of the Midwestern Psychological Association, Chicago, May 1992.

Lauterbach D, Vrana S. "Three Studies on the Reliability and Validity of a Self-Report Measure of Posttraumatic Stress Disorder." *Psychological Assessment*, 1996, 3 (1): 17–25.

Leary MR. "A Brief Version of the Fear of Negative Evaluation Scale." *Personality and Social Psychology Bulletin*, 1983, 9: 371–375.

LePage JP, Mogge NL, Sellers DG, DelBen K. "Line Staff Use of the Behavioral Observation System: Assessment of Depression Scale Validity and Cut Scores," *Depression and Anxiety*, 2003, 17 (4): 217–219.

Liebowitz MR. "Social Phobia." *Modern Problems of Pharmacopsychiatry*, 1987, 22: 141–173.

Liebowitz MR, Gorman JM, Fyer AJ, Dillon DJ, Klein DF. "Effects of Naloxone on Patients with Panic Attacks." *American Journal of Psychiatry*, 1984, 141: 995–997.

Linehan MM, Comtois KA, Brown MZ, Heard HL, Wagner A. "Suicide Attempt Self-Injury Interview (SASII): Development, Reliability, and Validity of a Scale to Assess Suicide Attempts and Intentional Self-Injury." *Psychological Assessment*, 2006, 18 (3): 303–312.

Linehan MM, Nielsen SL. "Assessment of Suicide Ideation and Parasuicide: Hopelessness and Social Desirability." *Journal of Consulting and Clinical Psychology*, 1981, 49: 773–775.

Lobello SG, Underhill AT, Fine PR. "The Reliability and Validity of the Life Satisfaction Index-A with Survivors of Traumatic Brain Injury." *Brain Injury*, 2004, 18 (11): 1127–1134.

Lohmann N. "Correlations of Life Satisfaction, Morale and Adjustment Measures." *Journal of Gerontology*, 1977, 32: 73–75.

Lopex-Pina JA, Sanchez-Meca J, Rosa-Alcazar AI. "The Hamilton Rating Scale for Depression: A Meta-Analytic Reliability Generalization Study." *International Journal of Clinical and Health Psychology*, 2009, 9 (1): 143–159.

Luby JL, Mrakotsky C, Heffelfinger A, Brown K, Spitznagel E. "Characteristics of Depressed Preschoolers With and Without Anhedonia: Evidence for a Melancholic Depressive Subtype in Young Children." *American Journal of Psychiatry*, 2004, 161 (11): 1998–2004.

Lund M, Foy DW, Sipprell RC, Strachan AM. "The Combat Exposure Scale: A Systematic Assessment of Trauma in the Vietnam War." *Journal of Clinical Psychology*, 1984, 40: 1323–1328.

Marmar CR, Weiss DS, Schelnger WE, Fairbank JA, et al. "Peritraumatic Dissociation and Posttraumatic Stress in Male Vietnam Theatre Veterans." *American Journal of Psychiatry*, 1994, 151: 902–907.

Marshall GN, Orlando M, Jaycox L. "Development and Validation of a Modified Version of the Peritraumatic Dissociative Experiences Questionnaire." *Psychological Assessment*, 2002, 14 (2): 123–134.

Marshall MB, Bagby RM. "The Incremental Validity and Clinical Utility of the Mmpi-2 Infrequency Posttraumatic Stress Disorder Scale." *Assessment*, 2006, 13 (4): 417–429.

Mason BJ, Kocsis JH, Leon AC, et al. "Measurement of Severity and Treatment Respondents in Dysthymia." *Annals of General Psychiatry*, 1993, 23: 625–631.

Mathias CW, Greve KW, Bianchini KJ, Houston RJ, Crouch JA. "Detecting Malingered Neurocognitive Dysfunction Using the Reliable Digit Span in Traumatic Brain Injury." *Assessment*, 2002, 9 (3): 301–308.

McDevitt-Murphy ME, Weathers FW, Adkins JW. "The Use of the Trauma Symptom Inventory in the Assessment of PTSD Symptoms." *Journal of Traumatic Stress*, 2005, 18 (1): 63–67.

McDonald S, Calhoun P. "The Diagnostic Accuracy of the PTSD Checklist: A Critical Review." *Clinical Psychology Review*, 2010, 30 (8): 976–987.

McDonald SD, Beckham JC, Morey RA, Calhoun PS. "The Validity and Diagnostic Efficiency of the Davidson Trauma Scale in Military Veterans Who Have Served Since September 11th, 2001." *Journal of Anxiety Disorders*, 2009, 23 (2): 247–255.

McDonald SD, Beckham JC, Morey RA, Marx CE, Tupler LA, Calhoun PS. "Factorial Invariance of Posttraumatic Stress Disorder Symptoms Across Three Veteran Samples." *Journal of Traumatic Stress*, 2008, 21 (3): 309–317.

McKay C, Casey JE, Wertheimer J, Fichtenberg NL. "Reliability and Validity of the RBANS in a Traumatic Brain Injured Sample." *Archives of Clinical Neuropsychology*, 2007, 22 (1): 91–98.

McMillen JC, Fisher RH. "The Perceived Benefit Scales: Measuring Perceived Positive Life Changes After Negative Events." *Social Work Research*, 1998, 22: 173–186.

Means-Christensen AJ, Sherbourne CD, Roy-Byrne PP, Craske MG, Stein MB. "Using Five Questions to Screen for Five Common Mental Disorders in Primary Care: Diagnostic Accuracy of the Anxiety and Depression Detector." *General Hospital Psychiatry*, 2006, 28: 108–118.

Miller IW, Norman WH, Bishop SB, Dow MG. "The Modified Scale for Suicidal Ideation: Reliability and Validity." *Journal of Consulting and Clinical Psychology*, 1986, 54 (5): 724–725.

Mogge NL. "The Assessment of Depression Inventory (ADI): An Appraisal of Validity in an Inpatient Sample." *Depression and Anxiety*, 2006, 23 (7): 434–436.

Mogge NL, LePage JP. "The Assessment of Depression Inventory (ADI): A New Instrument Used to Measure Depression and to Detect Honesty of Response." *Depression and Anxiety*, 2004, 20: 107–113.

Mogge NL, Steinberg JS, Fremouw W, Messer J. "The Assessment of Depression Inventory (ADI): An Appraisal of Validity in an Outpatient Sample," *Depression and Anxiety*, 2008, 25 (1): 64–68.

Monga S, Birmaher B, Chiappetta L, Brent D, et al. "Screen for Child Anxiety-Related Emotional Disorders (SCARED): Convergent and Divergent Validity." *Depression and Anxiety*, 2000, 12: 85–91.

Montgomery SA, Asberg M. "A New Depression Scale Designed to Be Sensitive to Change." *British Journal of Psychiatry*, 1979, 132: 382–389.

Morey LC. *Personality Assessment Inventory: Professional Manual.* Tampa, FL: Psychological Assessment Resources, 1991.

Morris MK. *A Readiness Evaluation of Professional Filler System and Forces Command Nurses at Darnall Army Community Hospital, Fort Hood, Texas.* Academy of Health Sciences (Army) Fort Sam Houston TX Health Care Administration, August 2002. As of October 29, 2010: http://handle.dtic.mil/100.2/ADA420901

Morriss R, Leese M, Chatwin J, Baldwin D. "Inter-Rater Reliability of the Hamilton Depression Rating Scale as a Diagnostic and Outcome Measure of Depression in Primary Care." *Journal of Affective Disorders*, 2008, 111: 204–213.

Moss H. "Psychopathy, Aggression, and Family History in Male Veteran Substance Abuse Patients: A Factor Analytic Study." *Addictive Behaviors*, 1989, 14 (5): 565–570.

Mundt JC, Katzelnick DJ, Kennedy SH, Eisfeld BS, Bouffard BB, Greist JH. "Validation of an IVRS Version of the MADRS." *Journal of Psychiatric Research*, 2006, 40 (3): 243–246.

Murdock PH. *U.S. Army Nursing Readiness: A Field Administration of the Readiness Estimate and Deployability Index (READI) in the North Atlantic Regional Medical Command (NARMC).* Academy of Health Sciences (Army) Fort Sam Houston TX Health Care Administration, May 2001. As of October 18, 2011: http://www.dtic.mil/cgi-bin/GetTRDoc?Location=U2&doc=GetTRDoc.pdf&AD=ADA420981

Myers MG, Stein MB, Aarons GA. "Cross Validation of the Social Anxiety Scale for Adolescents in a High School Sample." *Journal of Anxiety Disorders*, 2002, 16 (2): 221–232.

Neese LE, Caroselli JS, Klaas P, High WM Jr., Becker LJ, Scheibel RS. "Neuropsychological Assessment and the Disability Rating Scale (DRS): A Concurrent Validity Study." *Brain Injury*, 2000, 14 (8): 719–724.

Nelson C, St. Cyr K, Weiser M, Gifford S, Gallimore J, Morningstar A. "Knowledge Gained from the Traumatic Brain Injury Screen—Implications for Treating Canadian Military Personnel." *Military Medicine*, 2011, 176 (2): 156–160.

Neugarten BL, Havinghurst RJ, Tobin SS. "The Measurement of Life Satisfaction." *Journal of Gerontology*, 1961, 16: 134–143.

Nguyen TD, Attkisson CC, Stegner BL. "Assessment of Patient Satisfaction: Development and Refinement of a Service Evaluation Questionnaire." *Evaluation and Program Planning*, 1983, 6: 299–314.

Nock MK, Holmberg EB, Photos VI, Michel BD. "Self-Injurious Thoughts and Behaviors Interview: Development, Reliability, and Validity in an Adolescent Sample." *Psychological Assessment*, 2007, 19 (3): 309–317.

Norris F, Perilla J, Murphy A. "Postdisaster Stress in the United States and Mexico: A Cross-Cultural Test of the Multicriterion Conceptual Model of Posttraumatic Stress Disorder." *Journal of Abnormal Psychology*, 2001, 110: 553–563.

Nye EC, Qualls CB, Katzman JW. "The Trauma Symptom Inventory: Factors Associated with Invalid Profiles in a Sample of Combat Veterans with Post-Traumatic Stress Disorder." *Military Medicine*, 2006, 171 (9): 857–860.

Nyhus E, Barcelo F. "The Wisconsin Card Sorting Test and the Cognitive Assessment of Prefrontal Executive Functions: A Critical Update." *Brain and Cognition*, 2009, 71: 437–451.

Olatunji BO, Sawchuk CN, Deacon BJ, Tolin DF, et al. "The Anxiety Sensitivity Profile Revisited: Factor Structure and Psychometric Properties in Two Nonclinical Samples." *Journal of Anxiety Disorders*, 2005, 19: 603–625.

Orsillo SM, Theodore-Oklota C, Luterek JA, Plumb JC. "The Development and Psychometric Evaluation of the Emotional Reactivity and Numbing Scale." *Journal of Nervous and Mental Disease*, 2007, 195: 830–836.

Osman A, Bagge CL, Gutierrez PM, Konick LC, Kopper BA, Barrios FX. "The Suicidal Behaviors Questionnaire-Revised (SBQ-R): Validation with Clinical and Nonclinical Samples." *Assessment*, 2001, 8 (4): 443–454.

Osman A, Gutierrez PM, Jiandani J, Kopper BA, et al. "A Preliminary Validation of the Positive and Negative Suicide Ideation (PANSI) Inventory with Normal Adolescent Samples." *Journal of Clinical Psychology*, 2003, 59 (4): 493–512.

Osman A, Gutierrez PM, Smith K, Fang Q, Lozano G, Devine A. "The Anxiety Sensitivity Index–3: Analyses of Dimensions, Reliability Estimates, and Correlates in Nonclinical Samples." *Journal of Personality Assessment*, 2010, 92 (1): 45–52.

Ozonoff S. "Reliability and Validity of the Wisconsin Card Sorting Test in Studies of Autism." *Neuropsychology*, 1995, 9 (4): 497–500.

Park CL, Cohen LH, Murch RL. "Assessment and Prediction of Stress-Related Growth." *Journal of Personality*, 1996, 64: 71–105.

Perraud S. "Development of the Depression Coping Self-Efficacy Scale (DCSES)." *Archives of Psychiatric Nursing*, 2000, 15: 276–284.

Perrin SG, Meiser-Stedman RA, Smith PA. "The Children's Revised Impact of Event Scale (CRIES): Validity as a Screening Instrument for PTSD." *Behavioural and Cognitive Psychotherapy*, 2005, 33 (4): 487–498.

Pressler SJ. "Measuring Depressive Symptoms in Heart Failure: Validity and Reliability of the Patient Health Questionnaire-8." *American Journal of Critical Care*, 2011, 20 (2): 146.

Prins A, Oimette PC, Kimerling R, Cameron RP, et al. "The Primary Care PTSD Screen (PC-PTSD) Development and Operating Characteristics." *Primary Care Psychiatry*, 2003, 9: 9–14.

Radloff L. "The CES-D Scale: A Self-Report Depression Scale for Research in the General Population." *Applied Psychological Measurement*, 1977, 1: 385–401.

Reineck C, Connelly L. *Readiness Instrument Psychometric Evaluation.* Annual and Final Report Tri-Service Nursing Research Program (Bethesda, MD) and the Henry M. Jackson Foundation for the Advancement of Military Medicine (Rockville, MD), 1999.

Reiss S, Peterson RA, Gursky DM, McNally RJ. "Anxiety Sensitivity, Anxiety Frequency and the Prediction of Fearfulness." *Behaviour Research and Therapy*, 1986, 24: 1–8.

Resnick HS, Foy DW, Donahoe CP, Miller EN. "Antisocial Behavior and Posttraumatic Stress Disorder in Vietnam Veterans." *Journal of Clinical Psychology*, 1989, 45: 860–866.

Reynolds WM. "Psychometric Characteristics of the Adult Suicidal Ideation Questionnaire in College Students." *Journal of Personality Assessment*, 1991, 56 (2): 289–207.

Rhew IC, Simpson K, Tracy M, Lymp J, et al. "Criterion Validity of the Short Mood and Feelings Questionnaire and One- and Two-Item Depression Screens in Young Adolescents," *Child and Adolescent Psychiatry and Mental Health*, 2010, 4 (1): 8.

Riley AW, Forrest CB, Rebok GW, Starfield B, et al. "The Child Report Form of the CHIP-Child Edition: Reliability and Validity." *Medical Care*, 2004, 42 (3): 221–231.

Riley AW, Forrest CB, Starfield B, Rebok GW, Robertson JA, Green BF. "The Parent Report Form of the CHIP-Child Edition: Reliability and Validity." *Medical Care*, 2004, 42 (3): 210–220.

Ritsher JB, Struening EL, Hellman F, Guardino M. "Internal Validity of an Anxiety Disorder Screening Instrument Across Five Ethnic Groups." *Psychiatry Research*, 2002, 111: 199–213.

Rodebaugh TL, Chambless DL, Terrill DR, Floyd M, Uhde T. "Convergent, Discriminant, and Criterion-Related Validity of the Social Phobia and Anxiety Inventory." *Depression and Anxiety*, 2000, 11 (1): 10–14.

Rosen CS, Drescher KD, Moos RH, Finney JW, Murphy RT, Gusman FD. "Six- and Ten-Item Indexes of Psychological Distress Based on the Symptom Checklist-90." *Assessment*, 2000, 7 (2): 103–111.

Rousson V, Gasser T, Seifert B. "Assessing Intrarater, Interrater and Test–Retest Reliability of Continuous Measurements." *Statistics in Medicine*, 2002, 21: 3431–3446.

Ruggiero KJ, Del Ben KS, Scotti JR, Rabalais AE. "Psychometric Properties of the PTSD Checklist Civilian Version." *Journal of Traumatic Stress*, 2003, 16 (5): 495–502.

Rush AJ, Giles DE, Schlesser MA, Fulton CL, Weissenburger J, Burns C. "The Inventory for Depressive Symptomatology (IDS): Preliminary Findings." *Psychiatry Research*, 1986, 18: 65–87.

Ryan J, Glass L. "Substitution of Supplementary Subtests for Core Subtests on Composite Reliability of WAIS-IV Indexes." *Psychological Reports*, 2010, 106 (1): 13–18.

Scher CD, Stein MB, Asmundson GJG, McCreary DR, Forde DR. "The Childhood Trauma Questionnaire in a Community Sample: Psychometric Properties and Normative Data." *Journal of Traumatic Stress*, 2001, 14 (4): 843–857.

Schmidt NB, Keough ME, Timpano KR, Richeyu JA. "Anxiety Sensitivity Profile: Predictive and Incremental Validity." *Journal of Anxiety Disorders*, 2008, 22 (7): 1180–1189.

Schneider RJ, Johnson JW. "Development and Validation of a Video-Based Social Knowledge Test for Junior Commissioned Army Officers." Presentation at the Personnel Decisions Research Institute, Minneapolis MN, 2004. As of April 6, 2011:
http://handle.dtic.mil/100.2/ADA433412

Schneider RJ, Johnson JW. "Direct and Indirect Predictors of Social Competence in United States Army Junior Commissioned Officers." Personnel Decisions Research Institutes, Inc. U.S Army Research Institute for the Behavioral and Social Sciences, 2005, Technical Report No. 1171.

Schoop LH, Herrman TD, Johnstone B, Callahan CD, Roudebush IS. "Two Abbreviated Versions of the Wechsler Adult Intelligence Scale-III: Validation Among Persons with Traumatic Brain Injury." *Rehabilitation Psychology*, 2001, 46 (3): 279–287.

Schultz LT, Heimberg RG, Rodebaugh TL, Schneier FR, Liebowitz MR, Telch MJ. "The Appraisal of Social Concerns Scale: Psychometric Validation with a Clinical Sample of Patients with Social Anxiety Disorder." *Behavior Therapy*, 2006, 37: 392–405.

Schwab KA, Baker G, Ivins BJ, Sluss-Tiller M, Lux W, Warden D. "The Brief Traumatic Brain Injury Screen (BTBIS): Investigating the Validity of a Self-Report Instrument for Detecting Traumatic Brain Injury (TBI) in Troops Returning from Deployment in Afghanistan and Iraq." *Neurology*, 2006, 66 (5) Supplement 2: A235.

Scoboria A, Ford JD, Lin HJ, Frisman LK. "Exploratory and Confirmatory Factor Analyses of the Structured Interview for Disorders of Extreme Stress." *Assessment*, 2008, 15 (4): 404–425.

Shear K, Belnap BH, Mazumdar S, Houck P, Rollman BL. "Generalized Anxiety Disorder Severity Scale (GADSS): A Preliminary Validation Study," *Depression and Anxiety*, 2006, 23 (2): 77–82.

Shear KM, Vander Bilt J, Rucci P, Stat D, et al. "Reliability and Validity of a Structured Interview Guide for the Hamilton Anxiety Rating Scale (SIGH-A)." *Depression and Anxiety*, 2001, 13: 166–178.

Sheeran T, Zimmerman M. "Screening for Posttraumatic Stress Disorder in a General Psychiatric Outpatient Setting." *Journal of Consulting and Clinical Psychology*, 2002, 70 (4): 961–966.

Silverman WK, Saavedra LM, Pina AA. "Test-Retest Reliability of Anxiety Symptoms and Diagnoses with the Anxiety Disorders Interview Schedule for DSM-IV: Child and Parent Versions." *Journal of the American Academy of Child and Adolescent Psychiatry*, 2001, 40 (8): 937–944.

Simeon D, Guralnick O, Schmediler J. "Development of a Depersonalization Severity Scale." *Journal of Traumatic Stress*, 2001, 14 (2): 341–349.

Smith GR, Kramer TL, Hollenberg JA, Mosley CL, Ross RL, Burnam A. "Validity of the Depression-Arkansas (D-ARK) Scale: A Tool for Measuring Major Depressive Disorder." *Mental Health Services Research*, 2002, 4 (3): 167–173.

Smith MD, Hagman JD. "Year 1 Assessment of the Unit Focused Stability Manning System." U.S. Army Research Institute for the Behavioral and Social Sciences. Final report August 2003–August 2004. As of November 2, 2010:
http://handle.dtic.mil/100.2/ADA428049

Smith MD, Hagman JD. "Year 2 Assessment of the Unit Focused Stability Manning System." U.S. Army Research Institute for the Behavioral and Social Sciences: Final report, August 2005–June 2006. Report date: July 2006. As of November 2, 2010:
http://handle.dtic.mil/100.2/ADA456217

Smith P, Perrin S, Dyregrov A, Yule W. "Principal Components Analysis of the Impact of Event Scale with Children in War." *Personality and Individual Differences*, 2003, 34: 315–322.

Spielberger C, Edwards C, Lushene R, Montuori J, Platzek D. *Preliminary Test Manual for the State-Trait Anxiety Inventory for Children.* Palo Alto, CA: Consulting Psychologists Press, 1973.

Spielberger CD, Gorsuch RL, Lushene R, Vagg PR, Jacobs GA. *Manual for the State-Trait Anxiety Inventory.* Palo Alto, CA: Consulting Psychologists Press, 1983.

Spielberger CD, Jacobs G, Crane R, Russell S, Westberry L, Barker E, et al. *Scoring Manual for the State-Trait Personality Inventory.* Tampa: University of South Florida, 1979.

Steinberg M. "Advances in the Clinical Assessment of Dissociation: The SCID-D-R." *Bulletin of the Menninger Clinic*, 2002, 64 (2): 146–163.

Steinberg M. *Interviewer's Guide to the Structured Clinical Interview for DSM-IV Dissociative Disorders-Revised (SCID-D-R).* Washington, DC: American Psychiatric Press, 1994.

Storch EA, Masia-Warner C, Dent HC, Roberti JW, Fisher PH. "Psychometric Evaluation of the Social Anxiety Scale for Adolescents and the Social Phobia and Anxiety Inventory for Children: Construct Validity and Normative Data." *Journal of Anxiety Disorders*, 2004, 18 (5): 665–679.

Struening EL, Pittman J, Welkowitz L, Guardino M, Hellman F. "Characteristics of Participants in the 1995–1996 National Anxiety Disorders Screening Day." Unpublished manuscript, New York State Psychiatric Institute, 1998.

Taylor S, Cox BJ. "Anxiety Sensitivity: Multiple Dimensions and Hierarchic Structure." *Behaviour Research and Therapy*, 1998, 36: 37–51.

Taylor S, Zvolensky MJ, Cox BJ, Deacon B, et al. "Robust Dimensions of Anxiety Sensitivity: Development and Initial Validation of the Anxiety Sensitivity Index–3." *Psychological Assessment*, 2007, 19: 176–188.

Tedeschi RG, Calhoun LG. "The Posttraumatic Growth Inventory: Measuring the Positive Legacy of Trauma." *Journal of Traumatic Stress*, 1996, 9: 455–471.

Telch MJ, Lucas RA, Smits JJ, Powers MB, Heimber RG, Hart T. "Appraisal of Social Concerns: A Cognitive Assessment Instrument for Social Phobia." *Depression and Anxiety*, 2004, 18: 217–224.

Temple RO, Zgaljardic DJ, Abreu BC, Seale GS, Ostir GV, Ottenbacher KJ. "Ecological Validity of the Neuropsychological Assessment Battery Screening Module in Post-Acute Brain Injury Rehabilitation." *Brain Injury*, 2009, 23 (1): 45–50.

Thoresen S, Tambs K, Hussain A, Heir T, Johansen VA, Bisson JI. "Brief Measure of Posttraumatic Stress Reactions: Impact of Event Scale-6." *Social Psychiatry and Psychiatric Epidemiology*, 2010, 45 (3): 405–412.

Tluczek A, Henriques JB, Brown RL. "Support for the Reliability and Validity of a Six-Item State Anxiety Scale Derived from the State-Trait Anxiety Inventory." *Journal of Nursing Measurement*, 2009, 17 (1): 19–28.

Tombaugh T. "Trail Making Test A and B: Normative Data Stratified by Age and Education." *Archives of Clinical Neuropsychology*, 2004, 19: 203–214.

Trivedi MH, Rush AJ, Ibrahim HM, Cardmody TJ, et al. "The Inventory of Depressive Symptomatology, Clinician Rating (IDS-C) and Self-Report (IDS-SR), and the Quick Inventory of Depressive Symptomatology, Clinician Rating (QIDS-C) and Self-Report (QIDS-SR) in Public Sector Patients with Mood Disorders: A Psychometric Evaluation." *Psychological Medicine*, 2004, 34: 73–82.

Tucker S, Brust S, Richardson B. "Validity of the Depression Coping Self-Efficacy Scale." *Archives of Psychiatric Nursing*, 2002, 16 (3): 125–133.

Turner SM, Beidel DC, Dancu CV, Stanley MA. "An Empirically Derived Inventory to Measure Social Fears and Anxiety: The Social Phobia and Anxiety Inventory." *Psychology Assessment*, 1998, 1: 35–40.

Vaishnavi S, Connor K, Davidson JR. "An Abbreviated Version of the Connor-Davidson Resilience Scale (CD-RISC), the CD-RISC2: Psychometric Properties and Applications in Psychopharmacological Trials." *Psychiatry Research*, 2007, 152: 293–297.

Veit CT, Ware Jr. JE. "The Structure of Psychological Distress and Well-Being in General Populations." *Journal of Consulting & Clinical Psychology*, 1983, 51 (5): 730–742.

Victorson DE, Enders CK, Burnett KF, Ouellette EA. "The Injury Distress Index: Development and Validation." *Archives of Physical Medicine and Rehabilitation*, 2008, 89 (10) 1893–1902.

Vogt D, Proctor S, King D, King L, Vasterling J. "Validation of Scales from the Deployment Risk and Resilience Inventory in a Sample of Operation Iraqi Freedom Veterans." *Assessment*, 2008, 15: 391–403.

Vrana S, Lauterbach D. "Prevalence of Traumatic Stress and Post-Traumatic Psychological Symptoms in a Nonclinical Sample of College Students." *Journal of Traumatic Stress*, 1994, 7: 289–301.

Wagner S, Helmreich I, Dahmen N, Lieb K, Tadic A. "Reliability of Three Alternate Forms of the Trail Making Tests A and B." *Archives of Clinical Neuropsychology*, 2011, 26: 314–321.

Walter LJ, Meresman JF, Kramer TL, Evans RB. "The Depression-Arkansas Scale: A Validation Study of a New Brief Depression Scale in an HMO." *Journal of Clinical Psychology*, 2003, 59 (4): 465–481.

Ware J, Kosinski M, Keller SD. "A 12-Item Short-Form Health Survey: Construction of Scales and Preliminary Tests of Reliability and Validity." *Medical Care*, 1996, 34 (3): 220–233.

Ware JE, Manning WG, Duan N, Wells KB, Newhouse JP. "Health Status and Use of Outpatient Mental Health Services." *American Psychologist*, 1984, 39: 1090–1100.

Watson D, Clark LA. "The Mood and Anxiety Symptom Questionnaire." Unpublished manuscript, University of Iowa, Department of Psychology, 1995.

Watson D, Clark LA, Tellegen A. "Development and Validation of Brief Measures of Positive and Negative Affect: The PANAS Scales." *Journal of Personality and Social Psychology*, 1988, 54 (6): 1063–1070.

Watson D, O'Hara MW, Chmielewski M, McDade-Montez EA, et al. "Further Validation of the IDAS: Evidence of Convergent, Discriminant, Criterion, and Incremental Validity." *Psychological Assessment*, 2008, 20 (3): 248–259.

Watson D, O'Hara MW, Simms LJ, Kotov R, et al. "Development and Validation of the Inventory of Depression and Anxiety Symptoms (IDAS)." *Psychological Assessment*, 2007, 19: 253–268.

Watson D, Weber K, Assemheimer JS, Clark LA, Strauss ME, McCormick RA. "Testing a Tripartite Model: I. Evaluating the Convergent and Discriminant Validity of Anxiety and Depression Symptom Scales." *Journal of Abnormal Psychology*, 1995, 104 (1): 3–14.

Weathers F, Litz B, Herman D, Huska J, Keane T. "The PTSD Checklist (PCL): Reliability, Validity, and Diagnostic Utility." Paper presented at: 9th Annual Meeting of the International Society for Traumatic Stress Studies; October 1993; San Antonio, TX.

Wechsler D. *WAIS-R Manual: Wechsler Adult Intelligence Scale-Revised.* San Antonio, TX: Psychological Corporation, 1981.

Weeks JW, Heimberg RG, Fresco DM, Hart TA, Turk CL, Schneier FR, Liebowitz MR. "Empirical Validation and Psychometric Evaluation of the Brief Fear of Negative Evaluation Scale in Patients with Social Anxiety Disorder." *Psychological Assessment*, 2005, 17 (2): 179–190.

Weiss DS. "The Impact of Event Scale–Revised." In *Assessing Psychological Trauma and PTSD*, 2nd ed., JP Wilson, TM Keane (eds.). New York: Guilford Press, 2004.

Whyte J, Hart T, Bode RK, Malec JF. "The Moss Attention Rating Scale for Traumatic Brain Injury: Initial Psychometric Assessment." *Archives of Physical Medicine and Rehabilitation*, 2003, 84: 268–276.

Widom CS, Dutton MA, Czaja SJ, DuMont KA. "Development and Validation of a New Instrument to Assess Lifetime Trauma and Victimization History." *Journal of Traumatic Stress*, 2005, 18 (5): 519–531.

Wilde EA, McCauley SR, Kelly TM, Levin HS, et al. "Feasibility of the Neurological Outcome Scale for Traumatic Brain Injury (NOS-TBI) in Adults." *Journal of Neurotrauma*, 2010, 27: 975–981.

Wilde EA, McCauley SR, Kelly TM, Weyand AA, et al. "The Neurological Outcome Scale for Traumatic Brain Injury (NOS-TBI): I. Construct Validity." *Journal of Neurotrauma*, 2010, 27: 983–989.

Williams JBW, Kobak KA. "Development and Reliability of a Structured Interview Guide for the Montgomery-Asberg Depression Rating Scale (SIGMA)." *British Journal of Psychiatry*, 2008, 192: 52–56.

Williamson DE, Birmaher B, Ryan ND, Shiffrin TP, et al. "The Stressful Life Events Schedule for Children and Adolescents: Development and Validation." *Psychiatry Research*, 2003, 119 (3): 225–241.

Wolf EJ, Miller MW, Orazem RJ, Weierich MR, et al. "The MMPI-2 Restructured Clinical Scales in the Assessment of Posttraumatic Stress Disorder and Comorbid Disorders." *Psychological Assessment*, 2008, 20 (4): 327–340.

Wood JJ, Piacentini JC, Bergman RL, McCracken J, Barrios V. "Concurrent Validity of the Anxiety Disorders Section of the Anxiety Disorders Interview Schedule for DSM-IV: Child and Parent Versions," *Journal of Clinical and Child Adolescent Psychology*, 2002, 31 (3): 335–342.

Wright KD, Asmundson GJ, McCreary DR, Scher C, Hami S, Stein MB. "Factorial Validity of the Childhood Trauma Questionnaire in Men and Women." *Depression and Anxiety*, 2001, 13 (4): 179–183.

Youngstrom EA, Findling RL, Calabrese JR. "Effects of Adolescent Manic Symptoms on Agreement Between Youth, Parent, and Teacher Ratings of Behavior Problems." *Journal of Affective Disorders*, 2004, 82: 5–16.

Youngstrom EA, Findling RL, Danielson CK, Calabrese JR. "Discriminative Validity of Parent Report of Hypomanic and Depressive Symptoms on the General Behavior Inventory." *Psychological Assessment*, 2001, 13 (2): 267–276.

Yule W. "Anxiety, Depression, and Posttraumatic Stress Disorder in Children." In *The NFER Child Portfolio*. I Sclare (ed.). Windsor, England: NFER-Nelson, 1997.

Zgaljardic DJ, Temple RO. "Reliability and Validity of the Neuropsychological Assessment Battery-Screening Module (NAB-SM) in a Sample of Patients with Moderate-to-Severe Acquired Brain Injury." *Applied Neuropsychology*, 2010, 17(1): 27–36.

Zhang N, Zhang Y, Wu K, Zhu Z, Dyregrov A. "Factor Structure of the Children's Revised Impact of Event Scale Among Children and Adolescents Who Survived the 2008 Sichuan Earthquake in China." *Development and Aging*, 2011, 52: 236–241.

Zimmerman M, Mattia JI. "The Psychiatric Diagnostic Screening Questionnaire: Development, Reliability and Validity." *Comprehensive Psychiatry*, 2001, 42 (3): 175–189.

Zimmerman M, Posternak MA, McGlinchey J, Friedman M, Attiullah N, Boerescu D. "Validity of a Self-Report Depression Symptom Scale for Identifying Remission in Depressed Outpatients." *Comprehensive Psychiatry*, 2006, 47: 185–188.

Zimmerman M, Ruggero CJ, Chelminski I, Young D, et al. "Developing Brief Scales for Use in Clinical Practice: The Reliability and Validity of Single-Item Self-Report Measures of Depression Symptom Severity, Psychosocial Impairment Due to Depression, and Quality of Life." *Journal of Clinical Psychiatry*, 2006, 67 (10): 1536–1541.

Zohar AH, Shen G, Dycian A, Pauls D, et al. "The Military Life Scale: A Measure of Perceived Stress and Support in the Israeli Defense Force." *Israel Journal of Psychiatry & Related Sciences*, 2004, 41 (1): 33–44.

Zullig KJ, Pun S, Patton JM, Ubbes VA. "Reliability of the 2005 Middle School Youth Risk Behavior Survey." *Journal of Adolescent Health*, 2006, 29: 856–860.

List of Measures Included in the RAND Online Measure Repository

Acute Stress Checklist for Children (ASC-Kids)
Adolescent Cognitive Style Questionnaire (ACSQ)
Adult Suicidal Ideation Questionnaire (ASIQ)
Anxiety and Depression Detector (ADD)
Anxiety Disorders Interview Schedule (ADIS)
Anxiety Sensitivity Index–3 (ASI-3)
Anxiety Sensitivity Profile–22 Item Version (ASP-22)
Appraisal of Social Concerns Scale (ASC)
Army Post-Deployment Reintegration Scale (APDRS)
Assessment of Depression Inventory (ADI)
Beck Hopelessness Scale (BHS)
Beck Scale for Suicide Ideation (SSI)
Behavior and Symptom Identification Scale (BASIS-32)
Behavioral Observation System (BOS)
Bipolar Inventory of Symptoms Scale (BISS)
Brief Measures of Positive and Negative Affect (PANAS)
Brief Traumatic Brain Injury Screen (BTBIS)
California Psychological Inventory–Depression (CPI-D)
Center for Epidemiologic Studies Depression Scale (CES-D)
Changes in Outlook Questionnaire (CiOQ)
Changes in Outlook Questionnaire–Short Form (CiOQ-SF)
Child Health and Illness Profile–Child Edition, Child Report Form (CHIP-CE/CRF)
Child Health and Illness Profile–Child Edition, Parent Report Form (CHIP-CE/PRF)
Childhood Trauma Questionnaire (CTQ)
Children's Revised Impact of Event Scale–8 Item Version (CRIES-8)
Children's Revised Impact of Event Scale–13 Item Version (CRIES-13)
Clinically Useful Depression Outcome Scale (CUDOS)
Clinician-Administered PTSD Scale (CAPS)
CNS Vital Signs Battery (CNSVS)
Cognitive Style Questionnaire (CSQ)
Cohesion Questionnaire–Brigade Survey (CQ-BS)
Cohesion Questionnaire–Company Survey (CQ-CS)
Combat Exposure Scale (CES)
Composite International Diagnostic Interview (CIDI) – PTSD Module

Concussion Resolution Index (CRI)

Connor-Davidson Resilience Scale (CD-RISC) – 10 Item Version

Connor-Davidson Resilience Scale (CD-RISC) – 25 Item Version

Connor-Davidson Resilience Scale (CD-RISC2) – 2 Item Version

Cornell Dysthymia Rating Scale (CDRS)

Davidson Trauma Scale (DTS)

Depersonalization Severity Scale (DSS)

Deployment Risk and Resilience Inventory (DRRI)

Depression Arkansas Scale (D-ARK)

Depression Coping Self-Efficacy Scale (DCSES)

Disability Rating Scale (DRS)

Dispositional Resilience Scale–15 Item Version (DRS15)

Distressing Event Questionnaire 1 (DEQ 1)

Distressing Event Questionnaire 2 (DEQ 2)

Emotional Reactivity and Numbing Scale (ERNS)

Fear of Negative Evaluation–Brief Version (FNEB)

General Behavior Inventory–Parent Report (GBI-P)

Generalized Anxiety Disorder Severity Scale (GADSS)

Global Assessment Scale (GAS)

Global Assessment Tool (GAT)

Hamilton Rating of Depression Scale/Montgomery Asberg Depression Rating Scale Interview (HMI)

Hamilton Rating Scale for Anxiety (HAMA)

Hamilton Rating Scale for Depression (HAMD)

Impact of Event Scale (IES)

Impact of Event Scale–Revised (IES-R)

Impact of Event Scale–6 Item Version (IES-6)

Injury Distress Index (IDI)

Integrated Delivery System Consultation Assessment Tool (IDS-CAT)

Interactive Voice Response Montgomery Asberg Depression Rating Scale (IRV MADRS)

Interview for Mood and Anxiety Symptoms (IMAS)

Inventory of Depression and Anxiety Symptoms (IDAS)

Inventory of Depression and Anxiety Symptoms–Clinical Rating (IDAS-CR)

Inventory of Depressive Symptomatology, Clinician Rating (IDS-C)

Inventory of Depressive Symptomatology, Self Report (IDS-SR)

Joint Mental Health Advisory Team 7 Survey (J-MHAT 7)

Joint Mental Health Advisory Team 7 Survey (J-MHAT 7) – Barriers and Stigma Scale

Liebowitz Social Anxiety Scale (LSAS)

Life Satisfaction Index–A (LSI)

Lifetime Trauma and Victimization History (LTVH)

Los Angeles Symptom Checklist (LASC)

Mental Health Inventory (MHI)

Military Life Scale (MLS)

Minnesota Multiphasic Personality Inventory–2 (MMPI-2)

Mississippi PTSD Scale–Revised (M-PTSD R)

Mississippi Scale for Combat-Related PTSD (M-PTSD)

Modified Scale for Suicidal Ideation (MSSI)
Montgomery Asberg Depression Rating Scale (MADRS)
Mood and Anxiety Symptoms Questionnaire (MASQ)
Mood and Feelings Questionnaire–Child (MFQ-C)
Mood and Feelings Questionnaire–Parent Version (MFQ-P)
Mood and Feelings Questionnaire–Single Item Child Version (MFQ-C1)
Mood and Feelings Questionnaire–Single Item Parent Version (MFQ-P1)
Mood and Feelings Questionnaire–2 Item Child Version (MFQ-C2)
Mood and Feelings Questionnaire–2 Item Parent Version (MFQ-P2)
Moss Attention Rating Scale (MARS)
My Mood Monitor Checklist (M-3)
National Anxiety Disorder Screening Day Instrument (NADSD)
Neurological Outcome Scale for Traumatic Brain Injury (NOS-TBI)
Neuropsych Questionnaire (NPQ) – Adult Version
Neuropsych Questionnaire–Short Form (NPQ-SF)
Neuropsychological Assessment Battery–Screening Module (NAB-SM)
Non-Traumatic Stressors Questionnaire (NTSQ)
Numeric Anxiety Scale (NAS)
Patient Health Questionnaire (PHQ-8)
Patient Health Questionnaire–9 Item Version (PHQ-9)
Patient Health Questionnaire–2 Item Version (PHQ-2)
Pediatric Inpatient Behavior Scale (PIBS)
Pediatric Quality of Life Enjoyment and Satisfaction Questionnaire (PQ-LES-Q)
Penn Inventory for Posttraumatic Stress Disorder (Penn Inventory)
Pentagon Post Disaster Health Assessment (PPDHA)
Peritraumatic Dissociative Experiences Questionnaire (PDEQ)
Peritraumatic Distress Inventory (PDI)
Personality Assessment Inventory (PAI)
Pittsburgh Sleep Quality Index Addendum for PTSD (PSQI-A)
Positive and Negative Suicide Ideation Inventory (PANSI)
Post-Deployment Readjustment Inventory (PDRI)
Posttraumatic Growth Inventory (PTGI)
Posttraumatic Stress Diagnostic Scale (PSDS)
Primary Care–PTSD Screen (PC-PTSD)
Psychiatric Diagnostic Screening Questionnaire (PDSQ)
PTSD Checklist (PCL)
PTSD Checklist–2 Item Version (PCL-2)
PTSD Checklist–3 Item Version (PCL-3)
PTSD Checklist–4 Item Version (PCL-4)
PTSD Checklist–6 Item Version (PCL-6)
PTSD Symptom Scale–Interview Version (PSS-I)
Purdue Posttraumatic Stress Disorder Scale, Revised (PPTSD-R)
Quick Inventory of Depressive Symptomatology, Clinician Rating (QIDS-C)
Quick Inventory of Depressive Symptomatology, Self-Report (QIDS-SR)
RAND Peritraumatic Dissociative Experiences Questionnaire (RAND PDEQ)
Readiness Estimate and Deployability Index (READI)

Readiness Estimate and Deployability Index Revised for Air Force Nurses (READI-R-AFRN)
Readiness Estimate and Deployability Index Revised for Air Force Nurses Short Form
      (READI-R-AFRN [SF])
Repeatable Battery for the Assessment of Neurological Status (RBANS)
Revised Child Anxiety and Depression Scale (RCADS)
Screen for Child Anxiety-Related Emotional Disorders (SCARED)
Screen for Posttraumatic Stress Symptoms (SPTSS)
Self-Harm and Behavior Questionnaire (SHBQ)
Self-Injurious Thoughts and Behavior Interview (SITBI)
Short-Form Health Survey–12 item (SF-12)
Short Form Health Survey–36 Item (SF-36)
Short Mood and Feelings Questionnaire–Child Version (SMFQ-C)
Short Mood and Feelings Questionnaire–Parent Version (SMFQ-P)
Short Screening Scale for PTSD
Single-Item Global Measures of the Severity of Depression (GSEVDEP)
Single-Item Global Psychological Functioning Questionnaire (GPF)
Single-Item Global Quality of Life Questionnaire (GQOL)
Social Anxiety Scale for Adolescents (SAS-A)
Social Anxiety Scale for Adolescents Revised (SAS-AR)
Social Knowledge Test (SKT)
Social Phobia and Anxiety Inventory (SPAI)
Social Phobia and Anxiety Inventory for Children (SPAI-C)
State-Trait Anxiety Inventory (STAI)
Stressful Life Events Schedule–Child Version (SLES-C)
Structured Clinical Interview for DSM-IV Dissociative Disorders–Revised (SCID-D-R)
Structured Clinical Interview for DSM-IV PTSD Screening Module (SCID-PTSD)
Structured Interview for Disorders of Extreme Stress–Revised (SIDES-R)
Structured Interview Guide for the Hamilton Anxiety Scale (SIGH-A)
Structured Interview Guide for the Montgomery Asberg Depression Rating Scale (SIGMA)
Suicidal Behaviors Questionnaire–Revised (SBQ-R)
Suicidal Behaviors Questionnaire–Single Item (SBQ -1)
Suicide Attempt Self-Injury Interview (SASII)
Symptom Checklist–6 Item Version (SCL-6)
Symptom Checklist–10 Item Version (SCL-10)
Symptom Checklist–10 Item Version, Revised (SCL-10R)
Symptom Checklist–90–Revised PTSD Subscale (SCL-90-R)
Trails Making Test A and B (TMT)
Trauma Symptom Inventory (TSI)
Traumatic Events Questionnaire (TEQ)
Traumatic Life Events Questionnaire 2 (TLEQ 2)
Traumatic Life Events Questionnaire 3 (TLEQ 3)
Type D Scale–14 (DS14)
Veterans RAND 12 Item Health Survey (VR-12)
Veterans RAND 36 Item Health Survey (VR-36)
Wechsler Adult Intelligence Scale–III Block Design (WAIS-III/BD7)
Wechsler Adult Intelligence Scale–III Matrix Reasoning (WAIS-III/MR7)

Wechsler Adult Intelligence Scale IV (WAIS-IV)
Wechsler Memory Scale IV (WMS-IV)
Wisconsin Card Sorting Test (WCST)
Youth Risk Behavior Survey–2005 Middle School Version (MSYRBS)

Data Abstraction Form

Table E.1

Elements Abstracted from Each Article	Brief Description of Each Element	Response Options
General Information on the Measure		
Name of measure	The full or official name of the measure	Name and abbreviation
Reference(s)	The full reference information for each article on this measure. This could include multiple references.	References and a checkbox for "no other supporting articles"
Brief summary of the purpose of the measure	One to two sentences describing (1) the number of items in the measure, (2) how it is administered, and (3) what it is trying to measure	Brief summary
Measure domain	A list of the following domains being captured by the measure: 1. PTSD 2. Depression 3. Anxiety 4. TBI 5. Suicidal thoughts 6. Resiliency 7. Stress and coping, which includes measures of general stress and coping styles or skills 8. Exposure to traumatic events 9. Force readiness, which includes measures that assess whether service members are psychologically ready to be deployed 10. Unit cohesion. Domains reflect areas captured by scales or stand-alone subscales, not single items.	Multiple choice from the list of domains; more than one domain could be checked for each measure
Age group(s)	The age group that the measure was tested with: 1. Adults (18 years and older) 2. Adolescents or children. If the measure was used with adolescents or children, the mean or range of ages (e.g., 4–6 years) was included.	Multiple choice from list. Measures could be applicable to both adults and adolescents or children. There were also two integer fields, one minimum and one maximum to capture age ranges.
Used with a military population?	Whether or not one of the articles about this measure shows that the measure has ever been used with any military population.	Yes or no

Table E.1—Continued

Elements Abstracted from Each Article	Brief Description of Each Element	Response Options
Measure Administration		
Method of administration	A description of how the measure is administered: 1. Survey questionnaire (pen and paper), includes questionnaires, inventories, and checklists 2. Survey questionnaire (online) 3. Structured interview 4. Semi-structured interview 5. Observation rating form 6. Other (please describe) 7. No information available.	Multiple choice from the list of methods; more than one method could be selected for a single measure
Respondent	A description of who answers the questions in the measure: 1. Self-administered 2. Caregiver completing information about their child 3. Child self-report 4. Other (please describe) 5. No information available.	Multiple choice from the list of populations
Scoring the Measure		
Clinical cutoff score	Whether or not the measure has a clinical cutoff score, and what the clinical cutoff score(s) is.	Yes or no, and a description of the clinical cutoff score(s), if available
Number of items	The total number of items on the measure	Integer field; a "no information available" option
Measure subscales	Whether the measure has subscales, and a list and brief description of each, including the number of items per subscale. A subscale is a grouping on individual items that when considered together provide information about the same characteristic.	Yes or no, and a description of sub-scales (if applicable)
Response options and anchors	One or two sentences that describe the response options and anchors for each scale that comprises the measure (e.g., 1 [not at all] to 7 [very much]). If there are multiple scales or subscales, the response options and anchors for each scale are described.	A description of response options and anchors, and a "no information available" option
Reliability and Validity of the Measure		
Sample size (n)	The range of sample sizes included in the different studies regarding this measure from the smallest to the largest. If one population has been studied, only a single sample size is included.	Two integer fields, one minimum and one maximum to capture range, and a "no information available" option
Reliability testing	The range of reliability scores on the measure (from lowest to highest) across all studies included in the repository. Reliability was commonly reported as Cronbach's alpha, test-retest reliability, or internal consistency.	A description of reliability and a "no information available" option
Validity testing	The overall correlation scores between this and other measures. Validity was commonly established by correlating the measure with other similar measures (divergent validity). For screening and assessment measures, validity was also established by examining sensitivity and specificity (determining if the measure identifies individuals it is supposed to identify without identifying individuals it is not supposed to identify).	A description of validity and a "no information available" option

Table E.1—Continued

Elements Abstracted from Each Article	Brief Description of Each Element	Response Options
Locating the Measure		
How to obtain a copy of the measure	A description of how potential users can obtain a copy of the measure. For example, a complete copy of the measure may be available as published in one of the references, upon request from a specific publisher or available for download from a specific website. If measures were available on a specific website, a link to the actual measure was included.	A description of how to obtain the measure
Fees to use the measure	Whether there was a fee to use the measure, and a description of how much it costs to use the measure (e.g., $5/per person), if applicable.	Yes or no, and a description of the cost of the measure, if applicable
Measure Background		
Developer of the measure	A description of who developed the measure, including the original reference to the earliest publication of the measure we could locate.	A reference and a "no information available" option
Year the measure was originally developed	The year the measure was first released for use.	An integer box for the year and a "no information available" option
History of measure	A brief description of previous versions of the measure that were referenced in the reviewed articles. If this is the first version of the measure, it is specified here.	A description of previous versions of the measures and a "no information available" option
Related measures	The names of other versions of the measure (e.g., short form, additional language forms) included in the measure repository. If there are no other related measures in the measure repository, it is specified here.	A description of other versions of the measure in the repository and a "no information available" option

Glossary

Military Terms

force health readiness

The ability of United States military forces to optimize and protect the psychological and physical health of service members and their families through policies and programs across all phases of deployment. It is operationalized through a partnership between the service members who make up the force, their leaders at all levels, and health care planners and providers. Force health protection and readiness is also referred to as force protection, force preservation, or force preservation and readiness. (Office of the Deputy Assistant Secretary of Defense, 2011)

unit cohesion

The bonding together of members of an organization in such a way as to sustain their will and commitment to each other, their unit, and the mission. (Powell et al., 2006)

Clinical Terms

clinical assessment

A measure administered by a clinician or trained professional for the purpose of providing a diagnosis or informing a treatment plan.

screening

A measure used to identify at-risk populations.

self-administered measure

A subject provides information about himself or herself, such as on a questionnaire or in an interview. (Leary, 1995)

surveillance

A type of measure used to determine the prevalence of a problem in a given population (e.g., a measure used to determine the proportion of service members affected by depression).

Research Method Terms

reliability

The consistency or dependability of a measurement procedure or the extent to which a measured variable is free from random error. (Leary, 1995; Stangor, 2004; Pelham and Blanton, 2007)

validity

The extent to which a measurement procedure actually measures what it is intended to measure. (Leary, 1995)

Brief Guide to Interpreting Measure Reliability and Validity in the RAND Online Measure Repository

When selecting an appropriate measure, it is critical to understand whether that measure is both reliable and valid for the population you intend to use it with. It is important to remember that reliability and validity information in the ROMR is only for the population described in the ROMR. Following is some information to help with interpreting the reliability and validity information in the ROMR.

What Is Reliability?

Reliability is defined as the consistency or dependability of a measurement procedure or the extent to which a measured variable is free from random error (Leary, 1995; Stangor, 2004; Pelham and Blanton, 2007).

There are several types of reliability, including:

- **Inter-rater reliability:** used to assess the degree to which different raters/observers give consistent estimates of the same phenomenon
- **Test-retest reliability:** used to assess the consistency of a measure from one time to another
- **Internal consistency reliability:** used to assess the consistency of results across items within a test (Rousson, Gasser, and Seifert, 2002).

Several types of statistics are used to assess reliability including correlations, Cronbach's alpha, and Cohen's kappa. Reliability statistics are generally reported somewhere between 0.00 (no reliability) and 1.00 (perfect reliability). Most of the time, if two measures are compared side by side, the one with the reliability statistic closest to 1.00 is the more reliable measure. It is important to note that the number of items in a measure can influence its reliability. Users should consider both the number of items and reliability information when making a decision about which measure is most appropriate (Leary, 1995; Stangor, 2004; Pelham and Blanton, 2007; Rousson, Gasser, and Seifert, 2002).

What Is Validity?

Validity is defined as the extent to which a measurement procedure actually measures what it is intended to measure (Leary, 1995).

There are several types of validity, including:

- **Criterion validity:** used to assess the extent to which the measure actually captures the phenomenon it is trying to measure (i.e., the criterion) by comparing (or correlating) it with other measures of the same construct
- **Content validity:** used to assess the extent to which the test content covers a representative sample of the behavior domain to be measured
- **Predictive validity:** used to assess the extent to which the measure can predict (or correlate with) other measures of the same construct that are measured at some time in the future (Leary, 1995; Rousson, Gasser, and Seifert, 2002).

Statistics can be used as an indicator of validity. For example, to establish criterion validity, a measure would be correlated with another measure of the same construct and the correlation coefficient would represent the measure's criterion validity. Similar to reliability statistics, the correlation can range from 0.00 (no correlation) to 1.00 (perfect correlation), with higher correlations indicating a higher level of criterion validity (Leary, 1995). It is important to note the sample size in the article's publishing information on validity of the measure. Larger sample size generally provides more confidence that the measure has been validated using a representative sample of the target population. Users should consider both the sample size and validity information when making a decision about which measure is most appropriate.

Brief User Guide for the RAND Online Measure Repository

Getting to the ROMR

How do I get to the ROMR?
The ROMR is available at http://militaryhealth.rand.org/innovative-practices/measures.html

Do I need a password or to register to use the ROMR?
No, the ROMR is free for anyone to use.

Searching for Measures

What filters can I use to help find the measures I'm looking for?
The ROMR filters measures by

- Age
- Specific clinical domains such as depression, PTSD, or TBI
- Previous use with a military population
- Cost of purchasing the measure
- Number of items in the measure
- Whether the measure is intended to be self-administered or must be administered by a clinician or trained professional
- Respondent (e.g., an individual or caregiver responding about their child).

Can I search for a specific measure by name or a specific keyword?
Yes, the ROMR allows you to search by keyword or name using a free text field. Enter the name of the measure or keyword into the "Keyword" search box and click on the "Go" button.

Using Search Results

Can I compare measures side by side?
Yes, to compare measures side by side, click the check box next to the measures you want to compare and then click on the "Compare selected" button.

Is there a glossary to help me understand what is meant by certain words or domains included in the ROMR?

Yes, a glossary that defines the key terms used in the ROMR is available online at http://militaryhealth.rand.org/innovative-practices/measures.html

Some of the search results get cut off midsentence. How do I see the full text?

Clicking on the text that says "Read More" will show the full text.

References

Chandra A, Lara-Cinisomo S, Jaycox L, Tanielian T, Burns R, Ruder T, Han B. "Children on the Homefront: The Experiences of Children from Military Families." *Pediatrics*, 2001, 125 (1): 16–25.

Defense Health Board Task Force on Mental Health, *An Achievable Vision: Report of the Department of Defense Task Force on Mental Health*. Falls Church, VA: Defense Health Board, 2007.

"Innovative Practices for Psychological Health and Traumatic Brain Injury," RAND Corporation Center for Military Health Policy Research, undated. As of November 22, 2011:
http://www.rand.org/multi/military/innovative-practices.html

Leary MR. *Introduction to Behavioral Research Methods*, 2nd ed. Belmont, CA: Brooks/Cole, 1995.

Levin, A. "Major Study Will Assess 'What Works' in PTSD Care." *Psychiatric News*, 2011, 46 (7): 4–5.

Office of the Deputy Assistant Secretary of Defense, Force Health Protection and Readiness, *Force Readiness and Health Assurance Resources*. As of May 10, 2011:
http://forcereadiness.fhpr.osd.mil/home.aspx

Pelham BW, Blanton H. *Conducting Research in Psychology: Measuring the Weight of Smoke*. Belmont, CA: Brooks/Cole, 2007.

Powell K, D'Angelo C, Thornburg B, Nowak M. *Unit Cohesion Cross Leveling and Readiness: Viability and the Effects of Cross Leveling on Unit Readiness and the Impacts on Unit Cohesion*, Assistant Secretary of the Army (Manpower and Reserve Affairs), Publication No. ADA463157, November 2006. As of October 18, 2011:
http://oai.dtic.mil/oai/oai?verb=getRecord&metadataPrefix=html&identifier=ADA463157

Rousson V, Gasser T, Seifert B. "Assessing Intrarater, Interrater and Test–Retest Reliability of Continuous Measurements." *Statistics in Medicine*, 2002, 21: 3431–3446.

Stangor C. *Research Methods for the Behavioral Sciences*, 4th ed. Belmont, CA: Wadsworth, 2004.

Tanielian T, Jaycox L, eds. *Invisible Wounds of War*. Santa Monica, CA: RAND Corporation, MG-720, 2008. As of October 19, 2011:
http://www.rand.org/pubs/monographs/MG720.html

U.S. Government Accountability Office. *Performance Measurement and Evaluation: Definitions and Relationships*, Publication No. GAO-11-646SP, May 2005. As of October 19, 2011:
http://www.gao.gov/new.items/d05739sp.pdf

Weinick RM, Beckjord EB, Farmer CM, Martin LT, Gillen EM, Acosta JD, Fisher MP, Garnett J, Gonzalez G, Helmus TC, Jaycox LH, Reynolds KA, Salcedo N, Scharf DM. *Programs Addressing Psychological Health and Care for Traumatic Brain Injury Among U.S. Military Servicemembers and Their Families*. Santa Monica, CA: RAND Corporation, TR-950-OASD, 2011. As of November 22, 2011:
http://www.rand.org/pubs/technical_reports/TR950.html